# handbuilding
# pottery

# handbuilding
# pottery

HOW TO MAKE BEAUTIFUL POTS WITHOUT A
WHEEL, USING SIMPLE TECHNIQUES AT HOME

Josie Warshaw
photography by Stephen Brayne

LORENZ BOOKS

This edition is published by Lorenz Books

Lorenz Books is an imprint of Anness Publishing Ltd
Hermes House, 88–89 Blackfriars Road, London SE1 8HA
tel. 020 7401 2077; fax 020 7633 9499
www.lorenzbooks.com; info@anness.com

© Anness Publishing Ltd 2000, 2004

UK agent: The Manning Partnership Ltd, 6 The Old Dairy,
Melcombe Road, Bath BA2 3LR; tel. 01225 478444;
fax 01225 478440; sales@manning-partnership.co.uk

UK distributor: Grantham Book Services Ltd, Isaac Newton Way,
Alma Park Industrial Estate, Grantham, Lincs NG31 9SD;
tel. 01476 541080; fax 01476 541061; orders@gbs.tbs-ltd.co.uk

North American agent/distributor: National Book Network,
4501 Forbes Boulevard, Suite 200, Lanham, MD 20706;
tel. 301 459 3366; fax 301 429 5746; www.nbnbooks.com

Australian agent/distributor: Pan Macmillan Australia, Level 18,
St Martins Tower, 31 Market St, Sydney, NSW 2000;
tel. 1300 135 113; fax 1300 135 103;
customer.service@macmillan.com.au

New Zealand agent/distributor: David Bateman Ltd, 30 Tarndale
Grove, Off Bush Road, Albany, Auckland;
tel. (09) 415 7664; fax (09) 415 8892

Publisher: Joanna Lorenz
Project editor: Emma Clegg
Assistant editor: Martin Goldring
Consultant advisor: John Forde
US advisor: Nancy Selvage
Copy editor: Samantha Ward-Dutton
Projects copy editor: Gail Dixon-Smith
Reader: Joy Wotton
Designer: Celia Clay
Photographer: Stephen Brayne
Stylist: Diana Civil
Picture researcher: Pernilla Pearce
Illustrator: Robert Highton
Production: Yolande Denny

Previously published as *The Potter's Guide to Handbuilding*

10 9 8 7 6 5 4 3 2 1

NOTES

Learning a new craft can be tremendous fun, filling many
rewarding hours, but certain materials and equipment may
need to be handled with great care. The author and publisher
have made every effort to ensure that all the instructions in this
book are accurate and safe, but cannot accept liability for any
resultant injury, damage or loss to persons or property, however
it may arise.

As this book is designed for an international readership, terms
are occasionally bracketed to clarify the different specialist and
general terms. To avoid confusion, note that the first firing stage
in the UK is "biscuit firing", whereas it is the US "bisque firing".
Also in the UK an additional term "bisque" is used to mean a
particular firing that has a higher temperature than the glaze
firing that follows.

Captions for photographs of final work give the measurements
of the piece by height, unless otherwise specified.

# CONTENTS

# INTRODUCTION

Like many of my generation I came to clay initially through the influence of the Leach tradition. Bernard Leach's philosophy combined Eastern and Western ideas and was highly influential in shaping and building the studio pottery movement. He set a code of pottery practice that related both to the use of materials and to an appropriate pottery aesthetic. During formative years my attraction to clay was associated with the conventional ideas of the time about the material.

Working with clay seemed then to be accompanied by a resistance to the modern world of the synthetic or the mass produced. For myself, as an impressionable adolescent, my first clay mentor had an aura of oriental mysticism and accompanying spirituality. There was the seduction of the feel of the clay and the fascination of the processes – watching shapes take form on the wheel and seeing how the firing process transformed the colour and glaze. I found wood, oil, raku and gas firing particularly exciting, and could hardly wait for the tantalizing moment when the door of the kiln opened. To this day I still become excited when the temperature creeps low enough to ease open the door and take a peek inside. In time, this fascination turned to an understanding of the technical processes, but the challenge to explore, to invent and to express myself in my ceramic work continues.

Many of you may just be starting to work with ceramics and will be bringing with you fresh thinking and original creative approaches. This ensures that design and techniques are continually being injected with new ideas, unhindered by the often restricting oriental approach of Leach. The history of ceramics shows that the main processes and techniques have not changed, but that creative design has moved on. With hindsight we can see that it is the ideas of a particular period or

LEARNING TO WALK BY J WARSHAW, 1996.

culture that makes each historical development distinctive and recognizable, and that current thinking is central to how ceramics is valued and appreciated. In today's climate the choices are open and the contemporary potter is relatively free to interpret and explore ideas of aesthetics, subject, culture and materials in a personal way.

In recognition of this freedom I have tried to accommodate a wide range of techniques and technical possibilities to give methods of working with clay both for the beginner and for the more experienced potter, using clay as a medium for functional craftwork or for other purposes, such as sculptural to architectural work. I have avoided references to "pots" or "pottery" and instead have used the broader word "ceramics". Words such as "top edge", "additions of clay" and "base" can be interpreted in "pottery" terms as "rim", "handle" and "foot", but they also allow for the fact that working with clay does not only involve making pots. I have also tried to treat each area fairly, avoiding preferences towards individual methods or treatments, rather than implying that a certain form or surface is more important than another.

I hope that this book will serve as a practical manual for beginners and provide inspiration for more advanced potters, as well as providing a comprehensive update of the ceramic practice of today.

# CLAY: THE FUNDAMENTAL INGREDIENT

An abundant natural material, clay forms primarily around large granite outcrops, but is found all around us, in gardens, fields, and along riverbanks or roadsides. It contains alumina and silica, as well as small quantities of other minerals, and originates from feldspathic or granite rock, originally molten when the earth was formed, and transformed over millions of years by decomposition and weathering. Different proportions of the main and subsidiary minerals give each clay its individual qualities.

## Primary and secondary clays

There are two geological categories of clay: primary and secondary clays. Primary clays, which are found where they originally formed, include china clay or kaolin, a very pure clay used to give strength and whiteness to porcelain. Another is bentonite, which can be added to other clay to improve the plasticity of clay bodies. Secondary clays were deposited in sedimentary layers during their formation. Examples are ball clays, often blue or black in their unfired state, which also add plasticity and become white or buff after firing, and red clays that contain iron oxide, which acts as a flux that lowers the clay's firing temperature. This clay is used to make earthenware bricks, floor tiles and flowerpots.

## Altering a clay body

Materials can be added to a clay body to change and strengthen it. Altering a clay body in this way reduces the shrinkage rate and lessens the degree of stress during drying and firing.

You can mix clays at the dry or plastic stage to bring them to a required state of workability or openness and modify the colour and texture at the same time. Grog is a common material that is used to 'open' clay. It is a pre-fired clay that has been ground and prepared to different graded particle sizes ranging from dust to grit. You can add grogs to any clay to make it suitable for raku firing (see Glazing and Firing, raku firing), enabling the clay to withstand the thermal shock of dramatic temperature change. Grog will also bleed through a glaze at high temperatures to give a speckled effect. Ovenware clay bodies are designed with the addition of clay 'openers' such as lithium feldspar or talc in a silica-free body.

Other materials used to change a clay body include molochite, quartz, sand or fibrous material such as paper (see fibrous and paper clay techniques).

## Obtaining clay

Clay can be dug from the ground and prepared by slaking (see reclaiming clay), sieving and returning it to its plastic state. It is marginally easier to buy clay in dry, powdered individual materials which can then be mixed together. Both methods are labour-intensive and, in the case of preparing clay from dry materials, you will need to have access to specialist equipment.

Alternatively, it is possible to buy ready-made clay in a plastic state, packaged in sealed polythene bags, from a ceramic supplier. As you will also need to pay for the cost of delivery, then the more clay you buy the cheaper it will be per unit of weight. You can also buy or prepare different clays in a liquid state, called casting slip, for slip casting (see Making and Using Moulds, slip casting).

## Choosing a clay

Each clay has its own distinct make-up, resulting in a different handling quality, colour, temperature range and plasticity, or workability. These qualities are specified by ceramic suppliers and many will be willing to send small sample bags of clay through the post for you to test. The choice of clays is wide and you can also combine them, which will increase the possibilities further. Ready-prepared clays can be combined by weighing out the selected proportions of each clay and wedging and kneading them until thoroughly mixed (see preparing clay).

There are many things that you should find out about a clay that you are considering using. First of all, test its plasticity (see plasticity test). You should also establish whether a clay is suited to oxidized or reduced firing, if it is appropriate for your planned working methods, and what is its texture and fired colour, as well as its price. Most clays are suitable for any making technique, but there are some that are specifically designed for certain ones. A very plastic clay body designed and developed specifically for throwing purposes, for example, might not be suitable for the task of modelling fine detail where a smooth fine-particle clay will be more effective. If the correct clay is not selected, then you might find the forming clay stage to be a struggle, or encounter problems with the drying and firing processes.

Remember that changes can be made to the colour or texture of clay, as well as to its actual physical properties – namely its plasticity, workability and shrinkage rate. Alternatively, changes might be made to the clay body by either raising or lowering the degree of heat necessary in the kiln to achieve the required fired density.

The list of available clays is wide depending on the ceramic supplier you use and the range they have on offer (see suppliers and services).

## Handbuilding and modelling clays

These tend to be open clays to enable limited shrinkage and safe drying and firing, combined with adequate plasticity. A coarse or fine grog, or silver-sand addition can be introduced into a smooth clay body – depending on the texture that you require, add up to 20–30 per cent to prepare a clay in this way.

T-material is a handbuilding clay (only available in the UK) with a plastic coarse texture that fires to a white or off-white

colour. Its specially developed formula means that it is plastic to work with and has a low shrinkage rate, so does not warp or distort.

### Fibrous or paper clay

This is any clay to which fibres have been introduced. The raw clay is very strong (see fibrous and paper clay techniques), giving extra stability to fragile constructions. It is also easy to dry and to mend if broken or cracked.

### Casting clays

These clays must deflocculate, or break up into fine particles, to create casting slips. Clays that contain a large amount of iron or free alkali do not deflocculate and are not suitable for casting. The purer clays such as kaolin and ball clay, many buff burning stoneware clays and fire clay deflocculate and therefore cast well. A body that casts well is usually not plastic enough for throwing.

### Jigger and jolley clays

These clays are designed for use with the jigger and jolley technique (see Making and Using Moulds, jigger and jolley). They need to have moderate plasticity and should dry with a minimum of shrinkage and warpage. Trial and error is the best way of determining how a particular clay will perform with this making process.

### Throwing clays

These are dense, plastic and responsive. To increase the plasticity of a clay for throwing, up to 30 per cent ball clay is added (more than this will cause shrinkage and drying problems and also make the clay sticky). To give throwing clay extra staying power when standing on the wheel after being intensively worked, add up to 10 per cent grog or coarse clay at a particle size that will pass through a 30–60 mesh.

### Plasticity test

If you need to add grog or sand into plastic clay to reduce its shrinkage rate, you can calculate how much to add by weight or volume. To test how much grog can be kneaded into clay without losing its plasticity roll out a coil of clay to a width of about 2 cm ( ¾ in) and bend it to form a ring. If the clay cracks, it is

"short" and will be difficult to work. You can also measure plasticity by noting the amount of water you need to add to a measured amount of dry clay to take it to a suitable consistency. A finer clay will require more water than an open clay. If a clay contains more water, it will subsequently shrink more.

### The clay temperature range

Clay can be subdivided into five various temperature range groups:

- Earthenware has a maturing range of 1000–1180°C (1832–2156°F).

- Stoneware has a maturing range of 1200–1300°C (2192–2372°F).

- Porcelain has a maturing range of 1240–1350°C (2264–2462°F).

- Bone china has a maturing range of 1240–1250°C (2264–2282°F).

- Coloured clay has a maturing range of 1040–1220°C (1904–2228°F).

### Earthenware

Fired earthenware has a much lighter feel to higher fired clays, which have a more compact, dense quality. The colour of earthenware ranges from grey or white, to red, orange, buff, yellow and brown. Earthenware clay is abundant and available in nearly every part of the world. Red clay is a secondary clay found near the surface of the ground, which contains iron oxide, accounting for its relatively low firing temperature. Red clay is usually plastic and therefore suitable

for modelling, building, throwing or pressing. Light or white earthenware bodies are made by blending light burning clays, such as ball clay and china clay, or a stoneware clay with fluxes, such as talc frit or nepheline syenite, to give sufficient plasticity.

### Stoneware

The name "stoneware" comes from the dense, hard character of the clay body. The colour range for stoneware includes off-white, tan, grey and brown. Fired stoneware clay that is fully matured or vitrified has a water absorption rate of 3 per cent or less. The higher firing temperature of this clay means that adding a flux is less necessary. However this high temperature also means that feldspar can be used as a flux (as a 10–20 per cent addition) whenever necessary in order to lower the maturing temperature.

### Porcelain

The word "porcelain" is said to have evolved from "porcellno", a descriptive word given by Marco Polo in the 13th century to a translucent cowrie shell that looked like a little pig. This white-firing vitreous clay is translucent if worked to a thin wall and is fired to temperatures of 1240°C (2264°F) and above. It is made by combining white burning clays with feldspars and flint. The high firing temperature causes the particles to become dense and impervious and gives

EGYPTIAN DIARY
(32 x 7.5 CM / 12½ x 3 IN)
CLAY COLLAGE WALL PIECE, THIN PIECES OF COLOURED
CLAY ARE LAID ON TOP OF THE BASE SLAB
(SABINA TEUTEBERG).

CLOCKWISE FROM TOP LEFT: PLASTIC CLAY FOR BONE CHINA, COLOURED CLAY, PORCELAIN, STONEWARE AND EARTHENWARE.

fired porcelain similar qualities to glass. The ball clays, china clays or kaolin used in porcelain must be iron free and as plastic as possible. It is difficult to develop a porcelain for throwing, as the majority of white clays are characteristically non-plastic.

## Bone china

This porcelain clay is made from calcined ox bones, and is produced mainly in England and Japan. It was developed in the 18th century to meet the demand for a white translucent ware to compete with imported oriental porcelain. The clay body is difficult to work, being very short when plastic and fragile when dry. It is most suitable for slip casting,

but with the addition of up to 6 per cent bentonite can also be press moulded. Glaze firing is at a low temperature of 1080–1100°C (1976–2072°F).

## Coloured clay

Any clay can be coloured with oxide or stain additions, although a light or white coloured clay will give the best colour response. Adding colour will often lower a clay's firing temperature, so tests should be carried out.

## Maturing temperatures

Clay is often referred to as "maturing" or "vitrifying" at a certain temperature. This is the point at which a body reaches its maximum fired strength and compact-

ness, resulting from its progressive fusion during firing. Below this temperature the body is underfired, and will be weak and porous. Conversely, if a clay body is fired beyond its maturing temperature range then faults can occur, such as warping, bloating, collapsing or eventual transformation to a molten state. In the case of porcelain and bone china a state of near complete fusion is obtained resulting in their translucent qualities.

Research and consider carefully before selecting a clay – it should not only be suitable for your working method, but also have a temperature range to suit the glaze and the firing. Consider its specific properties throughout the design process.

## Clay shrinkage

One aspect of clay not always detailed in a supplier's catalogue is its shrinkage rate. Clays shrink at an approximate rate of 10–13 per cent from their raw to fired state, the highest shrinkage rate taking place from the leatherhard to the bone dry state. A higher shrinkage rate is very difficult to work with, so a fine-particle, dense clay can be "opened up" by adding materials, such as sand or grog (see preparing clay, kneading in additions) to reduce shrinkage. However, the grain structure of a clay is closely related to its plasticity or workability – the more open a clay, the less plastic it will become – so take care not to add too much grog.

Clays that are very dense can pose problems when attaching clay to clay, as in the case of slab building or joining handles. The high shrinkage rate increases the chances of cracks forming at joints during drying and firing. Surfaces you wish to remain flat can also warp or curl at the edges when dried and/or fired. Slow drying by wrapping the work in plastic and slow firing can get around some of the problems, but if this does not work, you will need to rethink your design or experiment with the composition of the clay body.

### Shrinkage test

Any clay body with or without added grog or other openers can be tested for shrinkage using the following method:

**1** Roll out a sheet of plastic clay approximately 1 x 2 cm (½ x ¾ in) thick and cut it into three strips about 14 x 4 cm (5½ x 1½ in).

**2** Accurately mark a line 10 cm (4 in) long with a sharp knife point and leave the strips to dry.

**3** Turn them frequently to avoid warping.

**4** Measure the length of the lines when the clay strips are bone dry.

**5** Fire the test pieces to their intended maturing temperature and measure the length of the lines of shrinkage again. If the final shrinkage rate from plastic to fired exceeds 10–13 per cent, i.e. if the line ends up at 9 cm (3½ in) or less, the clay body will be difficult to use and you will need to add grog (see Preparing Clay, kneading in additions).

THE PHOTOGRAPH ABOVE SHOWS THE SHRINKAGE TEST RESULTS FOR FIRED EARTHENWARE (TOP), DRY EARTHENWARE (MIDDLE) AND PLASTIC EARTHENWARE (BOTTOM). THE LINES MARKED ON THE PLASTIC CLAY ARE 10 CM (4 IN) LONG AND ARE MEASURED AFTER FIRING TO RECORD SHRINKAGE RATES.

### CALCULATING PERCENTAGE LINEAR SHRINKAGE

The following equations give the method of calculating shrinkage rates from plastic to dry, dry to fired and plastic to fired clay.

$$\% \text{ DRY SHRINKAGE (plastic to dry)} = \frac{\text{Plastic length} - \text{dry length}}{\text{Plastic length}} \times 100$$

$$\% \text{ FIRED SHRINKAGE (dry to fired)} = \frac{\text{Dry length} - \text{fired length}}{\text{Dry length}} \times 100$$

$$\% \text{ TOTAL SHRINKAGE (plastic to fired)} = \frac{\text{Plastic length} - \text{fired length}}{\text{Plastic length}} \times 100$$

## Fired maturity test

In some instances, such as if you are planning a piece of work that must resist taking in water to prevent frost damage, you will need to establish whether a clay has reached its fired maturity or full vitrification. To test the degree of water absorption on fired clay, weigh and mark for indentification three clay bars, which have been fired at the required temperatures to be tested. Boil them in water for two hours and weigh them again. Compare their weights – if there is no change, no water has been absorbed and the fired clay will be fully vitrified.

## Consistency

The consistency of a clay will affect the limits of the work to be made. A firmer clay will stand longer working time on the wheel or allow a higher wall to be built from joined coils. If additional elements are made from softer clay, this will allow a coil or handle to be attached with less pressure to a supporting form or a turned lid.

Clay should be soft enough to move but firm enough so that it does not stick to hands and surfaces. It does not take long to acquire a feel for the correct "give" and to assess the best consistency for using clay for the particular job in hand. If it is a struggle in either direction, wedge either softer or firmer clay, depending on which way the clay needs to go, into the mass.

Clay that is too wet can be kneaded on dry plaster slabs (see techniques, preparing clay) until enough moisture has been extracted and the clay is in a usable plastic state. If your clay is too firm and you have no spare soft clay, the only option is to leave the clay to go dry for reclaiming. You can save clay that is verging on being too firm to use by making holes in its mass, pouring in water, letting it soak in and then wedging the clay. Alternatively, you can leave the clay to soak and soften in a container of water.

## Clay storage

Clay can be stored for long periods of time in airtight plastic bags. If the bags get torn, seal them with strong plastic tape to prevent air reaching the clay. Clay can also be stored in airtight containers. For shorter storage periods wrap clay in sheets of plastic to prevent it from drying out. You can also use this system to store and retain work at the leatherhard stage.

## Using clay within the projects

The type of clay used in each of the projects is always specified and suitable alternatives are given. Weights of clay are given for some of the projects, although the exact quantity needed will depend on the scale and volume of work you are making. Remember that unused clay will keep for long periods as long as it is stored in airtight polythene or plastic.

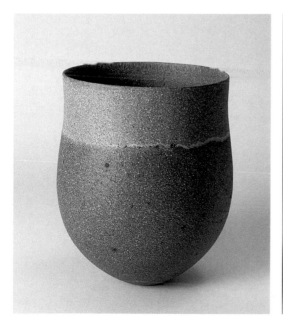

DARK POT WITH SLATE BLUE RIM (15.5 CM/6 IN)
T-MATERIAL COLOURED WITH OXIDES, PINCHED,
COILED AND OXIDIZED (JENNIFER LEE).

WHITE GARDEN (14 CM/5½ IN)
PORCELAIN, WHEEL THROWN, PAINTED WITH ACRYLIC
RESIST AND SUCCESSIVE LAYERS SPONGED AWAY, FIRED
UNGLAZED IN A REDUCING ATMOSPHERE (PETER LANE).

# EQUIPMENT

## PREPARING CLAY
Bought clay needs to go through the initial preparation processes of wedging and kneading, or alternatively pugging, before being ready to work with. In addition to this, and because about one third of plastic clay is water and clay delivery is paid for by weight, many makers who work with large quantities find it economical to make their own clay using dry materials or by refining local clay.

**For large quantities**

**A large clay blunger** is used in combination with a filter press for preparing large amounts of plastic clay. It contains a rotating vertical shaft with mounted paddles or blades. The dry materials are weighed then mixed with water in the blunger and passed through a vibrating sieve into a filter or clay press. This squeezes the water out of the liquid clay using pressure. The slabs of freshly made plastic clay are then peeled away from the cloths in the press to be stored or pugged ready for use.

**An electric clay mixer** is also used for preparing large quantities of clay, blending 500–750 kg (1000–1500 lbs) of dry materials into a clay body at a time. The materials are measured and added to the water in the mixer. This rotates and blends them to a plastic workable consistency.

**A small blunger** (shown above) is used for mixing clay with water to prepare liquid casting slips (see Making and Using Moulds, slip casting).

**A pugmill** is a metal barrel or cylinder, tapered at one end to a die. Clay is forced through the die by a rotating screw that consolidates and homogenizes the clay as it passes through. Clay that has been pugged can be used without wedging and kneading, as long as it is used immediately.

**For small quantities**

If you are preparing smaller quantities of clay, then you will need the following equipment:

1 A fixed bench from a heavy material, such as a concrete paving stone or slate. Ensure it is at a comfortable height for wedging – roughly as high as the top of your thigh.

2 A dry plaster slab (bat) for reconstituting wet clay can be simply made with potter's casting plaster (see Making and Using Moulds, preparing to pour plaster). Damage to plaster slabs should be avoided as plaster contaminates clay.

3 Scales and weights are also needed to weigh prepared clay into equal-sized balls.

4 A flat-headed paint scraper to clear any surplus clay on the bench (not shown).

5 Cutting wire for cutting the clay.

6 Plastic for storing prepared clay.

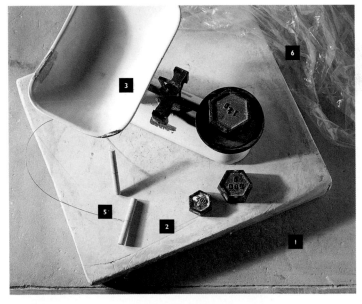

# TECHNIQUES
# PREPARING CLAY

Whatever you are using the clay for, you first need to ensure an even consistency throughout the clay's mass. This involves physically coaxing the clay into a homogenous state by wedging and kneading. A pugmill can be used for this process, dispensing with the need to wedge and knead the clay by hand, but many still prefer to wedge and knead after pugging to ensure that the clay particles are evenly aligned. A clay mass with an uneven consistency that has not been prepared well will be almost impossible to roll into an even slab or coil.

## Wedging clay

**1** To prepare the clay for kneading, the clay is first wedged by cutting the mass into pieces with a cutting wire. The pieces are cut so that they can be rearranged to break up the distribution of the firmer and softer clay.

**2** Lift one piece of clay at a time to shoulder height and slam it down onto the piece below. Reassemble and turn the faces into a new order to realign the firm and soft areas of clay within the mass. The new distribution of clay will now be easier to move during kneading.

## Kneading clay

Do not attempt to prepare too much clay at one time. While it is valuable to have thinking time in which to finalize ideas and get ready for the "hands on" work, kneading is a rhythmical physical exercise and should not be made overly strenuous. There are two types of kneading: spiral kneading and oxhead kneading. The names relate to the shape that the clay forms. Both methods are equally successful – choose the one that suits you.

For either method, stand with your feet astride and with one foot slightly in front of the other and use your body weight to rock into the clay.

**1A** Spiral kneading: turn the clay with one hand and, keeping your arm straight, use the heel of your other hand to apply a downward pressure by rocking your body. Rock the clay backwards and forwards, turning the mass by a hand's width and repeat the downward pressure completing an entire rotation of the mass.

**1B** Oxhead kneading: fold the clay in on itself, using the heel of both hands to exert a downward pressure. Rock the clay up with your fingers towards your body and then down again with the heels of your hands away from your body.

**2** Then cut the clay with a wire to check for lumps, air pockets and foreign bodies and if still uneven continue to knead, turning the clay by 45° before resuming.

This shows the spiral kneading technique with porcelain clay.

## Kneading in additions

Coloured clays for using in inlay, agate and millefiori work are prepared at the kneading stage by adding powdered stains and oxides. When making colour additions to clay at the kneading stage, you should decide what colour to use and at what strength you want to use it. Whether you are using colouring oxides or commercial stains, the colours are always added to a light- or white-coloured base clay body to obtain a good colour response.

Before kneading in stains and oxides, calculate the dry weight of both your colour addition and the clay to achieve a controlled colour. As 30 per cent of wet clay is water, 150 g (5 oz) of wet clay is equal to 100 g (3¾ oz) dry weight. Once the dry weight of your clay is calculated weigh the stain or oxide to give the desired percentage of colour shading. Moisten the stain before kneading to help distribute it evenly. Cut through the clay and check that the

additions are distributed evenly or unevenly as desired.

If you are using commercial stains for colouring clay, then remember that each stain will vary in its colour strength. Generally a darker colour will need a lower percentage of colour to give it a strong colour stain.

Experiment with colour additions of anything from 1–10 per cent. Note that blue oxides need only up to 2 per cent to give a strong blue.

You might also choose to carry out a number of fired test pieces to see the colour strength of the fired clay for different percentages of added colour.

As well as colour additions, materials such as sand, grog or mica can be added to plastic clay to create clay which, when fired, will be ovenproof. These materials can also be kneaded into the clay to reduce the shrinkage rate (see clay shrinkage) or to add texture or colour.

## Reclaiming clay

If clay has not been fired it can be reclaimed to be used again in its plastic state. To prepare clay for reconstitution you must first leave it to become bone dry – break or cut it into small pieces to allow maximum air contact.

**1** Once the clay is bone dry, "slake" it by covering it with water in a large, plastic bowl. Leave it to soak overnight until it becomes a thick slop.

**2** Any excess water that has not been absorbed should be removed the next day by carefully pouring it out or scooping it off.

**Note:** The length of time needed to reclaim clay will depend on how dry the plaster is, the room temperature and the consistency and amount of clay being reclaimed. You can cover the clay in plastic overnight to prevent it from drying out too much. When the clay has reached a manageable state, remove it from the plaster.

**3** Spread the slop in a 5–15 cm (2–6 in) thick layer on to dry plaster bats. It can then be turned to bring more surface area in contact with the plaster, which then absorbs moisture from the clay.

**4** If necessary, leave the clay slop on the plaster bats overnight to bring the clay consistency back to a firmness that is suitable for pugging or for wedging and kneading. Great care should be taken to ensure that pieces of plaster are not scraped or chipped off the plaster slab and therefore allowed to get into the clay, as this will contaminate it.

## TECHNIQUES
# FIBROUS AND PAPER CLAY The origins of this technique go back thousands

of years. As a mixture of rice husks, fresh cows' dung and clay, fibrous clay is still used in Asia as a

versatile building material for plastering walls and building large rice storage containers or for making

decorative shelving and alcoves.

■ Mixing clay with other fibrous materials, such as straw, fabric, hair or polyester fibre, extends its creative possibilities. Fibre clay greenware, or unfired clay, is very strong and this makes it easier to transport large or awkward pieces into the kiln. It is possible to attach wet or plastic fibre clay to dry and even biscuit (bisque) fired

clay. As the fibres in the clay create a strong bond there is no need to worry about cracks or breakages, and you can make large or otherwise difficult forms with carefree success!

Fibre clay is extremely versatile, warp free and light after firing. It can be thrown on the wheel, rolled to a paper thinness, printed, impregnated with

additives to give texture, or embedded with fired objects, such as mosaic or glass. String, leaves, wire and fabric, scrim or bandage can be soaked in fibre clay and used to build up forms by applying more layers with a paintbrush. The slop can be used for building up surfaces on to dry or leatherhard clay, giving increased strength to the structure.

### Making fibrous or paper clay

Fibre or paper pulp can be added to any clay to achieve fibrous clay. Shiny paper is not suitable as it will not break down sufficiently due to its waterproof latex resin content. Newspaper or cardboard egg cartons or fruit trays are most suitable. The print dye in newspaper will release into the pulp slop, but it can be washed off hands with soap and water and will burn out of finished work in the firing.

Preparing paper pulp is labour intensive. As a short cut, you can buy shredded paper pulp and cellulose fibre from ceramic suppliers. The cellulose fibre can be kneaded directly into plastic clay, or alternatively added to the slop if combined with other pulp or fibres.

**To make paper clay** you will need 7 or 8 half-dozen, cardboard egg cartons for each 25 kg (55 lb) plastic clay. Ensure that the amount of fibre or paper pulp never exceeds 50 per cent of the mixture.

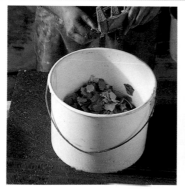

**1** Tear the egg cartons into small pieces. Soak them in hot water until they have softened, ideally overnight.

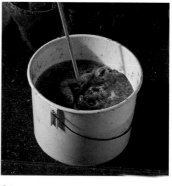

**2** Beat the soaked paper using a paint mixer attachment fixed to an electric drill. It is important to break down the paper fibres until they become a smooth even slop of roughly the same consistency as the clay slop you are going to add it to.

**3** Put the clay slop in a straight-sided bucket, level it off and stand a ruler in to measure its height. Work out how much paper slop can be added (a maximum of 50 per cent) and add the right amount of paper slop.

Continued ....

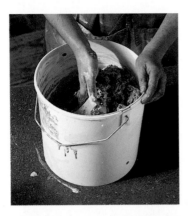

**4** Use your hands to mix the clay and paper slop thoroughly. Pour the mixed paper and clay slop on to plaster slabs in order to reclaim it into a plastic state. Once the slop has become firm, treat it in the same way as reclaimed clay.

### Storing fibrous or paper clay

Airtight bags or containers should be used for storing paper clay. The organic matter can become mouldy after a while and you can either reconstitute it or use it in this state. Apart from creating a smell during the making process, the mould will not affect the work itself.

### Firing fibrous or paper clay

Paper fibres burn in the kiln at approximately 300°C (572°F). The kiln must be fired slowly and will need good ventilation, as smoke will appear as the fibres ignite in the kiln. This is not a problem in an open-flued gas, wood or oil kiln, but an electric kiln will need to be well ventilated.

FROM THE SERIES ZIG ZAG
(40 CM/16 IN)
CLAYS, PAPER AND WIRE
SANDWICHED IN BLOTTING PAPER
AND PRINTED WITH CERAMIC
STAINS, OXIDIZED STONEWARE
(EWEN HENDERSON).

# HEALTH AND SAFETY

Many of the materials used in ceramics, particularly those for glazing, are toxic and should be handled with great care. Wearing and using the right equipment will protect you from any hazardous substances. Take precautions, especially when preparing dry materials, to prevent the inhalation of dust particles.

**¹** Apron.

**²** Protective gloves.

**³** Face mask that meets the appropriate particle size safety standards, BS6016 type 2 (dual cartridge respirator with a dust capturing prefilter).

**⁴** Safety goggles.

**⁵** Sponge for cleaning surfaces (avoiding dust creation).

### Take particular care with the following materials:

HIGHLY TOXIC
- Antimony
- Barium

USE WITH EXTREME CARE
- Lithium oxide sources – spodumene, lepidolite
- Boron sources – borax, boric acid
- Silica sources – quartz, flint, frits, feldspars, clays
- All of the colouring oxides and stains and underglazes

USE WITH CARE
- Aluminium oxide sources – feldspar, clay, calcined alumina, alumina hydrate
- Sodium oxide sources – soda feldspar, pearl ash, nitre
- Calcium oxide sources – whiting, dolomite
- Magnesium oxide sources – magnetite, dolomite, talc
- Zinc
- Strontium

LEAD
Lead is a hazardous substance. Many makers use lead in their glazes, while others prefer to avoid it. Some low-fired lead glazes are hazardous and should not be used in combination with copper or chromium oxide. These combinations are not suitable for the internal areas of domestic ware. In addition, all glaze wash water from work with lead glaze must be contained, collected, recycled or treated as toxic waste. Fritted leads should be used at all times. If you are unsure of the composition of a particular lead glaze you wish to use, you can take your work to a specialist laboratory for them to carry out a standard test for lead release on commercial ware. Lead should not be used when there are children around.

The book includes information and advice on using lead and some recipes with lead glazes. Ensure that you seek advice before using lead in your ceramic work and protect yourself with a face mask (respirator) and gloves that meet appropriate safety standards.

When beginning to use glazes, use only commercially prepared lead-safe glazes and never add copper to them. Use lead only if you have a safe way of collecting all waste water and having it collected as toxic waste.

### Safety tips

**1** Never inhale or ingest powders.

**2** Wear a safety mask (face respirator) and protective gloves when preparing glaze by mixing soluble materials. Wear gloves when using wet glaze. This prevents toxins being absorbed through the skin.

**3** Wear a safety mask (face respirator) when spraying glaze and colour, or if incising, rubbing or manipulating dry glaze before firing. Use proper extraction equipment when using a spray gun or airbrush.

**4** Avoid making dust at all times when preparing work or when cleaning up.

**5** Keep working areas clean and free from glaze. Vacuum floors (wet or dry) or wash them down with water to a drain. Use an absolute filter that collects very fine clay and chemical particles if vacuuming a dry floor. Avoid sweeping, and any activity that will create dust.

**6** Wear protective clothing and wash it regularly.

**7** Store materials in carefully labelled, fireproof lidded containers and always check the instructions on raw materials carefully.

**8** Do not store containers near kilns.

**9** Keep all ceramic materials away from children and pets.

**10** Never eat in your work area.

# WORKSHOP LAYOUT

The type, volume and scale of work that you make will be the dominant factor in deciding the layout, size and location of your studio or workshop space. It is not always possible to site a workshop on a ground floor, but there are obvious advantages to this when bringing in heavy materials or moving out large pieces of work. When starting from scratch, it may be necessary to compromise on your ideal workshop by acquiring expensive equipment in stages, prioritising which pieces are most important and therefore those that should be purchased first.

## The kiln

No matter how your work is made, there can be no finished ceramic work without the initial, and largest, financial outlay of a kiln (unless you use a communal one). It is possible to buy a second-hand electric kiln for considerably less than a new one, but check the model and number first and make sure you can still order replacement parts.

When purchasing a kiln for installation make sure there is adequate access through doorways, corridors or stairways to bring it to the intended site. All electric fired kilns, apart from the smallest, require an isolation switch and wiring in from the mains supply. Large electric kilns may require a three-phase electricity supply, which if not already present will add to the installation cost.

All kilns must be installed in a place that is ventilated near a window or extraction fan. Also consider whether its position will be practical for the type and quantity of work to be loaded into it. Fuel burning kilns require a flue or, unless located under an open-sided covering, a hood to collect fumes. Gas and oil kilns require a convenient source and access for fuel, as well as a safe storage place that is away from the direct heat of the kiln. Gas kilns can be adapted to portable gas where on-site delivery is not possible.

## Floor

Be practical – flooring should be hard wearing and smooth to allow for repeated and effective washing down. The ideal floor for heavy-duty or large-volume production is one that slopes down towards a drain. A heavy-duty vacuum cleaner with an adequate filter and the capacity to take up water is a good alternative.

## Water

Your main working space should ideally have a running water supply, preferably with hot water, which is particularly useful if you wish to attempt throwing techniques in the winter months. The sink should be large enough to wash out a bucket comfortably and its draining water should run into a settling or sediment tank (sink trap). This should be installed to take out heavy clay and glaze residue, preventing blockages to the drainage system and toxic materials entering the water system.

## Heating and ventilation

In cool conditions clay can be uninvitingly cold to work, glazes will freeze in their buckets and cold fingers are unable to carry out any task. This means that heating becomes essential to include for the worker as well as the work itself. However, overly heated studios during firings, in hot summer months, or those in the Southern Hemisphere can create adverse conditions of their own. In these conditions it becomes a race against time to apply handles or slip, as the work will move from leatherhard to dry in the brief moments taken to go to the fridge for a cool drink. In hot climates, organize some sort of ventilation, create areas that avoid direct sunlight and plan an open-sided, working space to keep conditions as comfortable as possible.

## Shelving

The type of shelving and storage you use will depend on the type of work you make. Makers of production ware will tend to choose an adjustable rack system. This means that long, narrow boards full of freshly made work can be easily transferred from the working area directly onto the drying rack. These boards or shelves can then be conveniently taken on and off the rack to turn the work for even drying. Large workshops in cold or wet climates will locate some form of heating near or under their drying racks to speed the drying process or prevent the wet work being frost damaged.

## Storage, surfaces and power

As well as storage for ongoing work, you will need a space for the finished work, to store clay and glaze materials and large containers. Other large pieces of equipment, such as slab rollers, extruders, pugmills and blungers should also be taken into consideration when planning space or electrical installation with isolation switches. If you need a spray booth, it must be located next to an outside wall to allow for extraction.

You will require one or more sturdy tables or work benches in the main clay area and an additional area or wedging bench for preparing clay. And do not forget to plan your lighting – you may wish to place the main working table or wheel next to a window.

## Organization

Plaster should always be kept separate from the main area used for working with clay to avoid contamination of the clay used for finished work. When trapped in the fired clay of a finished piece of work, plaster acts as a contaminant by absorbing and expanding. Any plaster that finds its way into a finished piece of work will irritatingly emerge from the fired clay or glazed surface months, sometimes years, later, leaving behind it an unwelcome scar. For this reason, ensure that all buckets and equipment used for plaster work are kept solely for plaster activities.

## Planning

Whatever size of workshop you are planning, whether you make buttons or large sculptural pieces, take time to visit the studios and workshop spaces of other makers. Look at their layout solutions and ask about their kilns and equipment before you decide on a final plan.

You could also consider renting or sharing a well-equipped studio. Such workspaces can often be found in the classified section of specialist magazines or on noticeboards in specialist shops and organizations. It is sometimes possible to hire the use of a kiln and, for short-term projects or small quantities of work, this may be adequate. Some craft associations offer grants for setting up a workshop and purchasing equipment.

## Studio layout

This photograph includes a wheel and its associated equipment, as these are some of the most difficult to accomodate in a studio. The kiln and the sink with settling tank (sink trap) are sited on the other side of the studio.

1 Electric wheel.

2 Pugmill.

3 Scales.

4 Light for use when working at wheel.

5 Wooden bats for use on the wheel.

6 Banding wheel.

7 Paint stripper gun.

8 Heater.

9 Preparing clay area and worksurface.

10 General worksurface.

11 Storage area with adjustable shelving for finished work and work in progress.

12 Underbench storage area for clay and other large-scale materials, such as plaster or mixed glazes.

13 Work in progress wrapped in plastic.

14 Practical flooring.

# DESIGN

Once you have developed an understanding of the physical making process, and some knowledge of

applied surfaces, you are then in a position to think about design. Whether you are making functional

ware, sculptural work or something that is a mixture of both, you should always start from an initial

design. This means choosing the surface, thinking about the scale, the type and form of firing, and

selecting a suitable clay to meet the requirements of what you want to make. Some design decisions will

rest on a vision of the finished piece, while others will emerge through the evolving progression of work,

or they will come through experimentation with ideas, forms and new materials.

■ Domestic ware designs will always be influenced by practical considerations unless they are to be deliberately disregarded in favour of an aesthetic. Is the shape of the handle suitable for grasping comfortably? Does the spout pour adequately? Does a lid stay on a teapot when it is poured? Will the glaze craze excessively and be unsuitable for domestic use? Once the practicalities are solved the form can be evolved and reassessed to tie in with your chosen methods. Design will involve meeting the practical considerations and working them out while keeping true to the desired visual appeal of a finished piece.

With sculptural or decorative work there is a wider freedom in the choice of design, but the constraints of the making process, materials and firing may sometimes impose limitations. Being ideas-led and overcoming the restraints of a material will often require experimentation and exploration until you can achieve the desired result. If a clay does not suit the limitations imposed by a chosen form you may need to rethink the material and change, for example, to a sandy or fibrous clay. If a surface does not match what you had planned, you will need to find a new decorating medium, glaze recipe or colour addition.

Drawings are not always sufficient when making a three-dimensional design that needs to be considered from all angles. It is a good idea to build a small-scale version, called a maquette, in clay or another material, such as cardboard, before embarking on a large piece of

work. A maquette is used as an accurate, physical reference for scale and points of change of direction and as a reference to the overall feel or mood of a piece. This allows you to view and plan the work from all possible angles and enables you to explore alternatives without wasting working time on a large piece.

With the current use of technology to aid the design process, a new generation of computer-literate designers is emerging. Computer design can be valuable when it is appropriately applied, but should not be used to supplant the "soul" of contact and knowledge of clay as a material.

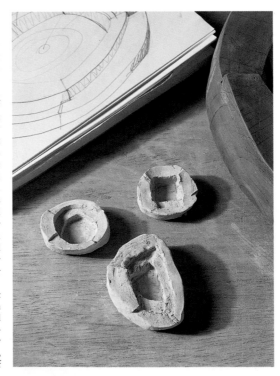

MAQUETTES AND
DRAWINGS ARE
IMPORTANT METHODS
OF EXPLORING AND
DEVELOPING IDEAS.

Forms can be transformed or accentuated with decoration that can give the work individual characteristics or act as a vehicle for self expression. Whatever your chosen idea, observation and thought are essential ingredients in order to make the idea work in practice. Many potters will make a prolonged study of a certain area before starting to make an actual piece of work. Images, ideas and objects can be collected or recorded by any process of drawing, painting, writing, collage, photography, video or documentation.

Designing on a three-dimensional surface opens up interesting possibilities for ways of arranging surface application. Inner and outer walls can be played against each other, changes in direction can be used as a transition point of the design, and the circuits of a design can be divided or made continuous.

THESE ORGANIC SURFACE SHAPES WERE CHOSEN TO BE IN KEEPING WITH THE ASYMMETRICAL FORM OF THE DISH AND WERE CAREFULLY PLACED UNTIL THEIR SPATIAL ARRANGEMENT LOOKED AND FELT RIGHT.

## Transferring designs to clay

The simplest and most immediate way to mark out a design on the surface of any biscuit (bisque) fired, dry or powdered glaze surfaces is to draw a pencil line freehand. Pencil marks will disappear in any type of firing. Add a little gum arabic or gum tragacanth in liquid form to an applied glaze as a binder or adhesive to toughen the powdered glaze surface for handling and application of a pencil line. The following techniques are suitable alternatives to freehand drawing.

Repeat designs or intricate designs can be indented into leatherhard clay using a pencil to follow traced or photocopied lines. Depending on the firmness of the clay this method can be used to leave a pleasingly rounded line as deep as the pressure applied to draw it. The indented line creates an inverted cloisonné look to the work when filled with colour.

To transfer a repeated design or one that is overly intricate and difficult to draw, use carbon copy paper to mark it out onto dry or biscuit (bisque) fired clay.

Pouncing is a useful and quick technique for transferring repeat designs to flat surfaces, such as tiles, to make a guideline for decorating with colour. This method can be used on a basic clay surface or on top of a powder glaze surface in preparation for onglaze decoration. The technique involves pushing lead graphite powder through holes in a stencil using a stiff brush or stencil brush.

# EQUIPMENT

**A WIDE RANGE OF EQUIPMENT IS INVOLVED IN THE CREATION OF CERAMICS,** FROM THE VARIOUS SPECIALIZED TYPES OF KILN, TO THE MORE EVERYDAY TOOLS THAT CAN MAKE ALL THE DIFFERENCE IN THE CREATIVE PROCESS. THIS CHAPTER DETAILS ALL THE TOOLS THAT ARE NEEDED FOR THE TECHNIQUES OF HANDBUILDING, MOULDMAKING, GLAZING AND FIRING.

# EQUIPMENT
# HANDBUILDING

Working efficiently and accomplishing a good finish to your work in clay is much easier when you have access to the correct tools. As well as those shown here, you will need a well lit, flat, level working area.

**1** A cloth for rolling out slabs.

**2** A rolling pin for rolling out slabs.

**3** Rolling slats or guides.

**4** Thin polythene (plastic) for wrapping work and maintaining leatherhard clay.

**5** Wooden boards for supporting work or larger boards for rolling out slabs.

**6** Rubber kidneys for smoothing, in different sizes and degrees of flexibility.

**7** An assortment of metal kidney shapes for paring, scraping and smoothing.

**8** A surgical scalpel is the sharpest knife available. Stocked in good art shops, they come with interchangeable blades.

**9** A potter's knife with a pointed tip that will not drag on clay.

**10** Hooped wire (trimming) tools for carving, modelling and hollowing out.

**11** Hardwood tools for modelling.

**12** Hole cutters make clean cuts to leatherhard clay.

**13** Plastic cards make ideal kidneys and can be cut to shape and filed to a profile.

**14** A paddle for tapping or beating soft clay.

**15** A forged steel tool for modelling and carving.

**16** A needle to pierce enclosed shapes.

**17** A harp (wire) for slicing slabs.

**18** A cutting wire for preparing clay or for cutting work free from a board.

**19** A trimmer enables the cutting of soft clay with one hand.

**20** A soft, natural sponge makes fewer ridges when wiping back any uneven clay.

**21** Banding wheels for turning work vary in weight and size – heavier ones give greater stability and momentum.

**22** Large pieces of foam are useful to support and protect awkward work (not shown).

**23** A slab roller makes rolling a large number of sheets of clay much easier (not shown).

The equipment above is available through standard pottery suppliers. The four items below are available from building suppliers.

**24** Fine-toothed hacksaw blades for paring and modelling.

**25** Curved and straight surform blades shave away clay and make straight edges.

**26** A countersink can be used with clay to countersink holes, as for woodworking.

**27** A paint stripper gun to speed-dry clay (a powerful hairdryer can be as effective)

## Extruding tools

**28** A wad box or extruder creates extruded shapes by forcing plastic clay through a die. The height of the box will dictate the maximum length.

**29** Various shaped dies are available to modify the shape of the extrusions.

**30** To extrude hollow shapes a metal plate is fixed to the centre of the die.

**31** An extrusion from a square shaped hollow die.

**32** A selection of handle extrusions.

**33** A clay gun for decorative extrusions.

# E Q U I P M E N T
## M O U L D M A K I N G Many straightforward plaster moulds, such as one piece press, hump or

sprig moulds, can be made with limited and easily obtainable equipment. Mould and model making at a

more advanced level, such as making and using block and case piece moulds and turned plaster models,

however, require a range of specialist tools and larger pieces of equipment.

■ If you have space, it is advisable to designate a separate area for plaster work as even small pieces of plaster that find their way into a finished piece can cause "blow outs", where plaster makes its way out of the fired clay. Keep moulds separate from clay and ensure that the working moulds are handled with care when in contact with clay, particularly when trimming the edges of pressed shapes.

Plaster working tools are prone to rust and will lose their edge unless they are well cared for. Always clean them with a knife blade or wire brush after use. Frequent applications of oil help prevent rusting.

A SEALED LATHE IS USED FOR TURNING PLASTER MODELS TO FIT THE WIDTH RESTRICTION OF THE LATHE.

A BANDSAW IS USED FOR CUTTING PLASTER MODELS AND MOULDS.

A WHIRLER (BANDING WHEEL) IS USED FOR TURNING WET PLASTER MODELS USING A HANDHELD OR BRIDGE FIXED TEMPLATE.

**1** An indelible pencil for marking plaster.

**2** Flexible plastic sheet, plaster sheets or slabs to make up side and base sets for containing plaster when poured for casting.

**3** String for securing side sets (retaining walls).

**4** Inner tube lining cut into strips for holding together assembled mould pieces.

**5** Bench scraper for cleaning off work surfaces and equipment.

**6** Profile former to shape clay or plaster.

**7** A steel hammer (a) and a rubber mallet (b) for releasing plaster models.

**8** Solid steel shock absorber disc to disperse hammer blows to plaster.

**9** Carpenter's saw to cut and scrape or smooth plaster.

**10** Surform blade to pare cast plaster.

**11** Cottle to form the sides of a cast

**12** Bristle brush (a), soft soap (b) and a sponge (c) for separating plaster piece moulds and plaster cast from plaster models.

**13** Plaster turning tools and forged steel serrated modelling tools for turning plaster.

**14** Straight edge and metal scrapers for screeding (spreading) wet plaster.

**15** Small spirit level (a), surface gauge (b), steel square (c) and callipers (d) for levelling, measuring and marking.

**16** Sandpaper for final smoothing of plaster surface (not shown).

**17**  Scales and a scoop for weighing plaster (not shown).

**18**  Wearing a face mask (respirator) will avoid the inhalation of plaster dust (not shown here – see health and safety).

## Additional equipment

For slip casting, a blunger is needed for preparing casting slip and a tray for collecting excess slip. For jigger and jolley techniques you will require a jigger or jolley arm fixed to the wheel head with a template former for forming soft clay on plaster moulds.

# EQUIPMENT
# GLAZE AND DECORATION

Both the basic glazing and decoration equipment, such as brushes or buckets, and the more specialist equipment, such as sieves or masks (respirators), are available from ceramic suppliers. Spraying equipment involves a greater financial outlay, and is unnecessary if your preferred methods of applying glaze and colour are by brush, dipping or pouring.

**Equipment for preparing ceramic colour and glaze**

Even if buying your glaze as powders ready made, there is often a certain amount of weighing and preparation involved. All the equipment listed here is a standard range, which will be essential for this stage of work.

**1** Accurate scales and weights for large (1a) and small (1b) quantities are used for weighing glaze ingredients, particularly colour additions or small quantities of test ingredients. When weighing out, check items off as you go in case of interruption.

**2** Sieves are used for sieving ceramic colour. Mesh sizes vary, measured by holes per square inch. An optimum for ceramic colour is a 60–80 size mesh. Test sieves (2a) are used for smaller amounts and large sieves (2b) for larger quantities.

**3** Sieve brush for pushing materials through a sieve.

**4** Support slats for supporting sieves over a bucket.

**5** Mortar and pestle for crushing stubborn materials before passing through a sieve and returning them to the mix.

**6** Bucket and a range of plastic ware suitable for safe, airtight storage and for transferring materials.

**7** Indelible pen for labelling buckets, as many mixed recipes look very similar once in slop form.

**Equipment for applying glazes**

**8** A spray gun (8a) and compressor (8b) are used with a spray booth to apply colour or glaze when a flat, even application or a diffused quality is required. They are useful when you have only a small quantity of glaze. A spray gun is linked to a compressor via a flexible air hose. Airbrushes can also be used to spray small areas of decorative colour.

**9** Glazing claw for gripping work when using a glaze that is susceptible to pouring and finger hold marks.

**10** Safety mask or respirator (see health and safety) and gloves (not shown).

**11** Brushes for applying glaze colour.

**12** Measuring jug (cup) for pouring or transferring glaze.

## Equipment for printing

Equipment for screen printing on ceramics is essentially the same as for screen printing on paper or fabric.

**13** Screen with hinged frame – using a screen attached to a board makes the screen printing process much easier to control.

**14** Silk screen.

**15** Squeegee for pulling colour across the silk screen.

**16** Liquid mediums, thinners and covercoats for oil-based colours.

**17** Thermoflot paper for making screened decals (or transfers).

## Lino cutting equipment

**18** Lino (linoleum block).

**19** Lino (linoleum) cutter

**20** Interchangeable blades for the lino (linoleum) cutter.

**21** Potter's tissue (ceramic tissue) for transferring a lino (linoleum) print to a clay surface.

## Brushes

There is a vast array of brushes on the market. Every brush has its own quality in terms of precision, spring, versatility of stroke and loading capacity, ranging from generous to resilient.

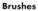
When decorating and applying colour, have a selection of different brush sizes and shapes at hand to choose from, To be able to select the right brush for the stroke, get to know the brushes that are available. Test a brush's load and stroke on a porous surface to find its "personality". Newspaper or a wooden board is good for this, and closely resemble the "draw" that biscuit (bisque) ware or powdered glaze exerts on a brush. What a flat test area will not give, though, is the feel of painting onto a curve.

Look after your brushes carefully and wash them after each use. This is essential when using wax resist and latex resist solution, which should never be allowed to dry on a brush. Store brushes with their heads straight.

**22** One stroke brushes can be used flat for laying on wide areas or can be drawn on their edge to make a fine line.

**23** Pointed writer for fine lines.

**24** The glaze mop's full, soft body will hold large quantities of colour.

**25** Traditional Japanese brushes are used for fine decorative work or calligraphy.

**26** Fine Japanese calligraphy brush.

**27** The traditional hake brush is soft haired for laying on large, flat areas of colour or slip.

**28** Fine liner brush.

The different brushes are used according to the types of stroke that they perform. All the brushes shown here are available in a variety of sizes.

# EQUIPMENT
# FIRING

Brick-built kilns all work on the same principle of an enclosed construction in which the work to be fired is placed. Radiated or combusted heat flows freely around the ware and is directed in its circulation or draught either through, down or up, or as a combination, towards a flue. The heat climbs at a controlled rate until a desired temperature has been reached.

## Kilns

The choice of whether to install a gas or electric kiln and whether it loads from the top or front is personal preference combined with practical factors, for example which fuel is available and affordable, the size of kiln you require and where it is to be located.

All kilns require adequate ventilation as firing creates noxious and often toxic fumes, so if yours is to be located indoors, it is essential to have fume extraction via a fan and/or a chimney hood. Reduction firings with gas, oil or wood-fired kilns produce carbon monoxide so in this case ensure that the kiln is sited outside or away from the main working area.

There are many different styles of kilns so it is advisable to take a good look at what is available as well as assessing all the practical factors (see Suppliers and Services).

This front loading kiln might typically be used by one person regularly firing quantities of production ware. Alternatively the cost of this essential piece of equipment could also be shared between those working in the same space.

Lightweight refractory bricks retained in a stainless steel casing provide efficient insulation on top loading kilns, making them economical to fire. Top loaders are lighter and therefore easier to move and transport than front-loading kilns. Some gas-fired top loaders are built in interlocking sections enabling the firing chamber to be adjusted according to the size or quantity of work making them economical to fire.

## Pyrometers

A pyrometer is an instrument that indicates the temperature of the firing chamber inside the kiln. It is housed outside the kiln and is linked to a thermocouple inside a porcelain sheath, which is fitted through the wall of the kiln and protrudes into the firing chamber. A thermocouple works by sensing heat in terms of the voltage passed across two wires in different metals that are joined together at one end. The greater the amount of heat applied to the junction, the greater will be the voltage generated by the wires. There are several types of thermocouple which means that temperature indicators and controllers have to be re-calibrated for each particular thermocouple type.

## Controllers

This piece of equipment controls the firing temperature of the kiln. There are various controllers on the market ranging from those that just provide a cut-off point at the final firing temperature to those that enable control over the entire firing cycle. The other points of the firing cycle that can be preset with a controller are the time firing begins (delay start), the set points at which the rate of temperature is increased, and also the rate of temperature increase (ramps). Other controller functions include the control of the latter or middle part of a firing called "soaking" where the kiln temperature is held at a fixed point for a measured amount of time.

## Raku Equipment

For pioneering potters, small raku kilns or large trolley loading kilns can be built to suit personal firing requirements. The designing and building of a kiln is a practical and viable solution requiring specialist high temperature materials and the necessary tools. Refractory bricks, ceramic fibre and aluminous cements and mortars are just a few of the materials necessary to withstand the high temperatures used in the firing process.

The basic eqipment for raku work is a raku kiln, gas burner and gas bottle (propane tank). A metal container filled with water is used for the rapid cooling of work, and a metal container filled with sawdust is used for immersing and reducing hot work

from the kiln. A pad of wire wool or a scrubbing brush is necessary to remove loose carbon deposits, and goggles are essential to protect the eyes. A pair of thick leather gloves is used for handling hot work, and finally tongs are used to move work in and out of the kiln.

## Kiln sitters and limit timers

Many top loading electric kilns are fitted with kiln sitters, which turn the kiln off at the end of a firing cycle. A small orton cone or minibar inside the kiln (see photograph far right) dictates the point at which a weighted switching device cuts off the kiln's electricity supply. The kiln sitter does not allow automatic soaking at the end of a firing cycle, but it can be manually set for firing by lifting the counterweight and pressing the button to reset the kiln energy regulators to a lower setting. The kiln sitter is a reliable way of programming the end of the firing cycle, with the advantage of being triggered by active heat or heatwork (see Glazing and Firing) rather than being triggered solely by temperature.

The limit timer controls the temperature at which the kiln is turned off.

A kiln sitter (automatic cut off device) is set with the appropriate minibar cone, which melts at the end temperature and releases the cut off weight.

## Gas burner and adjustment valve

Reduction in gas, oil or wood fired kilns is indicated by the length and type of flame you can see through the spy holes and flue. The burner's fuel intake and the secondary air supply are adjusted and the flue damper is partially closed to regulate the kiln's atmosphere until the correct reduction conditions occur. An oxidizing or neutral flame is blue, clear and straight, whereas a reduction flame is orange and curls and licks.

## Stilts, shelves, piers and racks

Kiln furniture is made from a high firing refractory material that can withstand high temperatures without warping. It is used for separating work in the kiln, while making full and economic use of the space in the firing chamber. Kiln shelves are stacked alternately on three tiers of kiln props (kiln bricks) set directly above one another at each layer. Stilts are used to support work with glazed bases to prevent contact with the kiln shelves. Flat objects such as tiles and plates require a lot of shelf space and are uneconomic to fire without the use of racks. A selection of kiln furniture is shown above, including a kiln shelf (at base), a tile rack (back left), kiln props (bricks) (far right) and stilts (foreground, middle left).

## Nichrome wire bead rack

The problem of how to fire glazed and Egyptian paste beads (which adhere to surfaces when fired) is removed with the use of a bead rack. Bead trees or racks fixed into clay supports can also be custom made with Nichrome wire, which you can buy from ceramic suppliers. Nichrome wire is the only wire that will withstand the high temperature of the kiln.

## Pyrometric cones

Not all kilns come well equipped with temperature controllers, so it is important to have an accurate indication of active heat or heatwork, as opposed to the temperature registering inside the kiln during firing. Pyrometric cones serve this function. These cones are numbered according to the temperature at which they melt and bend. They are placed as far into the firing chamber as possible in line with the view through, but avoiding draughts from, the spyhole.

A number of different ranges of cones exist, including Orton, Seger and Harrison in varying temperatures and corresponding numbers, which do not run consecutively. The different ranges can be intermixed within a set of cones.

# HANDBUILDING

**THERE ARE MANY PROCESSES INVOLVED IN POTTERY,** BUT THE ACTUAL PHYSICAL MANIPULATION OF CLAY IS CRUCIAL. THIS CHAPTER EXPLORES THE ESSENTIAL REPERTOIRE OF DIFFERENT HANDBUILDING TECHNIQUES INCLUDING: PINCHING, COILING, SLAB BUILDING AND EXTRUSION. METHODS OF DECORATING INTO CLAY, SUCH AS SPRIGGING, PIERCING AND BURNISHING ARE ALSO EXPLAINED IN DETAIL.

# TECHNIQUES

**PINCHING** The technique of pinching is one of the simplest ways of manipulating clay and as a result is often underestimated in its potential to create different surfaces or tensions. At the start pinched clay has a flaccid quality with a surface similar to overly ripe, dimpled fruit, but it can be transformed to a taut or precise form, full of vigour and life.

## Pinching

Always pinch out the bottom area of clay first, leaving the rim until last, to avoid cracks forming. If cracks do appear at the rim, smooth them down with a finger, smooth in a piece of soft clay, or cut the cracks away with the tip of a potter's knife.

**1** To start a pinched shape using prepared plastic clay (see preparing clay), take a ball that fits comfortably in your hand. Press your thumb down into its centre to within 5 mm (¼ in) of the ball's opposite wall.

**2** Starting at the deepest point, pinch the clay between your finger and thumb. Rotate the ball as you continue to pinch, moving up to the top edge while supporting the opened ball in your other hand. Turn and pinch with even pressure to reach the required wall thickness.

## Changing and manipulating a shape

**1** You can make an elongated shape in a similar way, but you roll the initial ball into a cone shape and pull the sides of the wall up over your thumb. Any ridges that form can be pinched out or removed once the shape is leatherhard.

**2** To shape a form outwards, stroke the inside with your finger tips while supporting the clay in the other hand. Check the profile of the shape all the way round as you do this. If the clay has been shaped beyond what you require, you can bring it back in while it is still soft.

**3** To shape a form inwards, gather or fold the wall and squeeze it together. V-shaped cuts can also be made to a rim, or leaf-shaped cuts to a bellied wall where unwanted bulges occur. The cut shapes are removed before pushing and smoothing the wall back together again.

**4** Top edges and walls can be pinched to a paper thinness to give a pinched shape a feeling of tension. It is often easier to wait until the shape has firmed before you finish the rim of a pinched shape. To level a rim, wait for the shape to become leatherhard and then cut the edge with a knife tip or grate it down with a surform blade. When it is level, pare the section of the rim with a hacksaw blade so it is even. Pinch the parts that need further thinning. Final paring to round, flatten or taper the rim can be done with a hacksaw blade or a metal kidney and then wiped with a damp sponge. Alternatively, you can leave shapes with a fat rim and add coils or slabs to give the shape a chunkier feel.

CLOSED BOWL WITH
CONVOLUTED MOUTH
(14 CM/5½ IN)
PORCELAIN, THROWN
AND PINCHED
(DEIRDRE BURNETT).

## Making a hollow enclosed shape

Made from two pinched cups, hollow, enclosed shapes can be manipulated while still soft. This joining technique can start a figuratively based piece of work or make a main or additional component of a piece.

**1** To join two pinched cups together leave a level, fat edge on each cup so there is enough excess clay to pull one edge over the other. The second cup should be slightly larger than the first to allow the rim edges to sit together and to allow for an overhang of clay on the second cup, which can be pulled over the edge of the first. Smear or pull the clay around the circumference of the seam line.

The trapped air inside the shape will keep it inflated while you continue to work. If it is not completely sealed the shape will buckle inwards or deflate, so seal a hole or weak point straight away with very soft clay.

**2** When it is completely sealed the enclosed hollow shape can be tapped, rolled or beaten with a paddle to finalize its form. Again, if the shape is punctured or feels weak at a particular point, ensure it is repaired before manipulating it further. Once leatherhard, the shape can be pared and smoothed.

**3** Before allowing the shape to become too dry, make a small hole with a needle to allow some of the air to escape. This will prevent the shape from cracking as it shrinks and dries.

## Using a pinched shape as a starting point

Pinched open and enclosed forms can be used as starting points to make components or to begin a piece of work.

A fat edge left on a pinched, open shape that is intended as a beginning for a coiled or soft slab piece, gives a good fixing surface from which to proceed. It can be thinned down once the join has been made.

Walls, joins and pinch marks can be pared and thinned on plastic clay using a hacksaw blade and a metal kidney. Support the wall with your non-working hand when applying pressure with tools. You may find it more comfortable to rest the shape in your lap to give it extra support. The clay can be worked while it is still plastic, but any last-stage finishing should be left until the clay is leatherhard.

**Note:** Remember to finish off the inside areas of a tall, narrow piece before it gets too high, as this may prevent you reaching inside. Pare the inside of a curved shape with a curved edge of a metal kidney and the outside with the flat edge. This will prevent flat ridges and scars from marring a final surface that is meant to be smooth.

### Leatherhard clay

In a cheese-like state of leatherhardness, recognised by its cold feel and firmness, the once soft clay can support the weight of further additions of applied clay without buckling or distorting. Leatherhard clay can still make a strong bond with any additional plastic clay applied using the score and slurry technique (see using slurry for joining slabs). It is also suitable for paring and smoothing work with tools and can support the weight and stress of applied coils, slabs, handles, footrings (feet) or other components.

### Pinching fibre clay

Pinched forms made from fibre clay can receive additions beyond the leatherhard stage until bone dry. Soak any dry surfaces with water first before applying further clay using the slurry and scoring technique (see using slurry for joining slabs).

RIDGED POT (25 CM / 10 IN)
PINCHED FORM IN PORCELAIN AND STONEWARE WITH
POWDERED MOLOCHITE MIX AND INLAID T-MATERIAL STARS.
STAINED BODY CLAY WITH BLACK IRON OXIDE, MANGANESE
OXIDE. RAKU FIRED AND REDUCED (JANE WALLER).
PHOTOGRAPH BY CRISPIN THOMAS.

# TECHNIQUES

## COILING

This fast, practical and versatile method can be used to construct complicated or simple forms. It permits a freedom to create large, imaginative, unrestricted forms that are built up in a series of stages and can be used in conjunction with any other techniques of forming clay. It is important to have a clear idea of the finished shape before you start to coil so that the size and shape of the base or beginning fits the scale and direction of the planned piece.

Everyone has their own particular style of making and attaching coils. Alternative methods for making coils to the one shown are extrusion (see extrusion) or cutting flattened strips or irregular shapes of flat clay from a rolled slab (see slab building). Some makers prefer to show the workings of the technique and not to pare away the pinch marks or join seams.

The wall can be made to look taut or flabby, chunky or thin, smooth or dimpled. There are no set rules, except that the coils or flattened pieces should be consistent along their entire length and that the coils are soft enough to join without having to apply unnecessary pressure, which could distort a soft supporting wall.

### Making coils

**1** Start by squeezing out a length of prepared plastic clay.

**2** Give yourself plenty of room on the working surface so the coil can be fully rolled while using your fingers to apply pressure where the coil is thick. You can make coils in bulk and store them in polythene (plastic) or roll them out as you progress with the work.

ADDING COILS TO THE FULL-BELLIED COILED POT (SEE PROJECT).

FULL-BELLIED COILED POT IN PROGRESS. COILS ARE PINCHED AS THEY ARE BUILT UP PRODUCING A DELICATE POT WALL (SARAH SCAMPTON).

## Building a wall

A coiled wall can start from a point or from the top edge of a flat or curved base, and it can be joined to an existing piece of leatherhard work made by an alternative method (see using slurry for joining slabs). The important thing to remember is that what you are coiling onto must be able to support the weight and pressure required to join the next coil. If the wall is soft and unable to support the applied weight, allow it to firm to leatherhard before carrying on. A little patience here will pay off as this will prevent the form from sagging, cracking or collapsing. Making changes of direction includes allowing the piece to firm at particular points before continuing to work.

If a wall is straight and vertical, you should place and join coils directly on top of each other. To direct a wall outwards, place and join the coils to the outer edge of the coil below. Conversely, to direct a wall inwards, place and join coils to the inner edge of the coil below.

When joining circuits of coils to build up a wall, it is helpful to turn the work on a banding wheel (see handbuilding equipment). Slurrying and scoring is unnecessary when joining soft plastic coils, unless you are joining the first coil to a base or continuing to coil a piece that has become leatherhard.

**1** When attaching the first coil, either to a flat or curved base made of plastic or leatherhard clay, you must first apply slurry and score the area using a pointed tool, such as a knife tip. This roughens the surface so that the applied coil will make a firm bond with the clay below. It is a good idea to slurry and score along the attaching edge of the first coil as well. Roughening both surfaces will knot the coil and clay surface together.

**2** Give the coil a slight wiggle and apply pressure as you lay it into place before tearing or cutting it to the correct length to encircle the shape.

**3** To join coils, smear down clay from the upper coil onto the base or coil below it, covering the seam line completely. Do this around the entire circumference both along the inner and the outer face of the wall. If you want the seams to show on the outer face of the wall, join from the inside wall only. As the coil is smeared onto the clay below, support the wall with your other hand so the pressure does not move the wall out of alignment. As long as the rhythmical joining strokes are consistent and evenly pressured the wall will remain under control as it begins to grow. Join the coils thoroughly: if the joins are weak the work is likely to crack on drying and firing.

**4** To even and reinforce a join while the clay is still plastic, use the curved edge of a serrated kidney on the inside of a curve.

**5** On all other areas use the toothed edge of a hacksaw blade. Alter the direction and angle of the tool to come into or over a curve of a wall without leaving flat ridges. Use sweeping motions with the tools to strengthen the coil joins and thin the wall, crossing the previous strokes diagonally.

## Heightening the wall

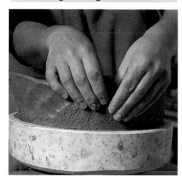

Pinch or pull up the wall evenly along its length to thin it out and add height. To make a paper-thin wall it is easier and quicker to add as thick a coil as you can and to continue to pinch it as far as the clay will allow. Individual makers develop their own methods of doing this.

## Making a wall smooth and even

After the piece has been left to to become leatherhard, pare and smooth down the walls again with greater pressure on the tools. When working on an enclosed form that is narrower than the width of your hand, smooth and finalize the internal walls after each coil circumference so you can avoid going back to the inside of a narrow shape. Inside such a shape it would be awkward, and sometimes impossible, to manoeuvre tools.

## Checking the shape

Every time you add a coil, check the shape and direction of the work. Closely inspect the entire "side-on" profile of the piece while turning it on a banding wheel, making sure it is exactly as required. Next, get a bird's eye view of the the top profile and check this as well. If the shape has gone askew, you can recover it as follows.

You can alter a bulge or an uneven profile by making cuts or tucks. The cuts can be slurried and scored on both meeting edges to join them back together or, if the clay is still soft and thick enough, the cuts can be smeared back together. An additional small piece of soft clay, slurried and scored over the join, will give added reinforcement and can be pared down once the join has firmed.

To bring the shape out on an edge, pinch the coil to lengthen it. A wall shape or slight depression that is still plastic can be eased out by stroking with your fingertips.

BAD ART BAD POTTERY
(60 CM/24 IN)
COILED EARTHENWARE, MARBLED
AND STENCILLED SLIP WITH INLAID
TEXT, SGRAFFITO DRAWING AND
PHOTO SILK SCREEN ENAMEL
TRANSFERS AND GOLD LUSTRE
(GRAYSON PERRY).

### Finishing rims and edges

Once you have finished building up the shape of the form, then attention can be given to finishing off the edges of the piece cleanly and neatly.

Use a surform blade on leatherhard work to level a rim or a top edge. You can also use a surform blade or knife tip to maintain a level working edge as the work progresses. Make sure your eyes are level with the edge to be cut. You may find it easier to measure and score a line first.

To create an even rim or top edge, pare down the top edge until the width is the same along its entire length. Bring the edge to a uniform thickness before shaping the edge or rim with a hacksaw blade. Apply pressure with the blade wherever the section is thickest while looking down onto the edge. Finish the edge or rim by removing any unwanted tool marks with a damp sponge.

TWISTING POT (30 CM/12 IN)
HANDBUILT STONEWARE, PINCHED FLATTENED COILS ADDED TO A PINCHED BASE, WITH NO SURFACE ALTERATION. THREE LAYERS OF GLAZES ARE USED – HIGH MAGNESIUM GLAZE, COBALT CARBONATE AND VANADIUM PENTOXIDE/IRON OXIDE MIXTURE WITH A TOP COAT OF HIGH BARIUM AND SILICON CARBIDE (JULIAN KING-SALTER).

### Working in stages

In most cases, it is usual to work on a coiled piece over a number of sittings, interspersed with waiting time while the work becomes firm enough to carry on. A paint stripper gun (see handbuilding equipment) is a useful piece of equipment to speed up the drying. If you decide to use one of these, keep it on the move to prevent any areas of clay becoming too dry. If the clay goes beyond the leatherhard stage and gains the characteristic pale colour of dry clay, the piece is ruined; the coils will not join and the walls will be hard and too brittle to work. To continue a piece over any number of working sessions, wrap it in plastic to keep it airtight and damp.

### Coiling fibre clay

The only time that there is no need to keep a piece in a leatherhard state is when working with fibre clay, which can still be worked when bone dry. Coils of plastic clay can be added to dry clay by first wetting the attachment area then slurrying and scoring in the usual way. Fibre clay can also be carved and cut at the bone-dry stage.

# TECHNIQUES
# SLAB BUILDING
There are two areas of slab building: leatherhard and soft slabbing, although, technically speaking, there will be times when you will need slabs of a certain flaccidity that fall somewhere between the two. Leatherhard slabs are required for work that has straight edges and planes and are worked with a precision and order similar to cutting and joining cardboard or wood. Soft slabbing is a more spontaneous and immediate method of working with slabs, suited to fluid, curved, folded or swollen forms. A slab that falls between the two will stand upright, but can still be curved.

Use prepared clay (see preparing clay) that is soft enough to move freely, but is not wet or sticky, when making leatherhard or soft clay slabs. Before rolling out prepared plastic clay work out the size and quantity you need. It is always a good idea to make a few extra slabs just in case.

Finer bodied clays have a tendency to warp when drying and firing so clays that are open (grogged, sandy or fibre clays) are more suitable for large, flat, planed slab work. The reduced shrinkage of an open clay also causes fewer problems with weak joins and lessens the risk of work pulling apart at the seams.

### Rolling fibre clay

Fibrous clay is particularly suitable for slab building as although it still shrinks on drying, any stress cracks can be repaired when the clay is bone dry.

### Rolling large quantities

For rolling out large quantities of slabs, use a slab roller (see handbuilding equipment). This is appropriate for large, architectural work, sculptural work or for preparing slabs for repeat production purposes.

### Rolling slabs

Work on a wooden board, a cloth or a sheet of plastic. If you do use either of the latter two, make sure there are no creases as these will imprint on your finished slab causing weakened fault lines.

Slabs can be rolled with or without the use of slats or guides. Without slats you can feel the distributed weight of a slab by picking it up and checking that its section is even throughout. Resting a rolling pin on slats can restrict the slab size by the length of the rolling pin. If you decide to use slats, choose a pair that are thick enough for the scale and feel of the piece you are making. When you are preparing to work with leatherhard slabs roll them out larger than they need to be. This is because a certain amount of "dry edge" surface will always be wasted because the edges tend to dry before the centre.

**1** Stand up to roll out a piece of clay to get your body weight behind the rolling pin. Press the clay out, pushing with the heel of your hand spreading the clay as far as it will go. Do this evenly over its entire surface.

**2** If you are using slats, rest the rolling pin ends on the slats and roll from the centre outwards. Push harder on the rolling pin where the clay is highest and continue until the clay will not spread any further. Lift the clay at its edges to put a pocket of air under the clay so it will free up and move again. Repeat the process, crossing previous rolls diagonally until you have an evenly rolled slab to the thickness required.

CURVED VASE (28 CM/11 IN)
RED EARTHENWARE CLAY, BUILT WITH
LEATHERHARD SLABS, DECORATED WITH
SLIPS AND SAWDUST FIRED. THE VASE IS
GLAZED INTERNALLY AND IS THEREFORE
NON-POROUS (TESSA WOLFE-MURRAY).

## Harp-cutting slabs

Instead of rolling out slabs, you can slice them out of a solid mass of prepared clay using a harp cutter (U-shaped rod).

■ Make sure the block of prepared clay is sitting on a flat surface large enough to site the ends of the harp level with the bottom face of the block. Draw the wire of the harp through the block from top to bottom, one slab at a time. After each cut, move the rings of the harp wire down a notch to cut the next slab.

## Making fibre-clay slabs

When using fibre clay, you can spread the slop on to make sheets or slabs in preparation for printing, decorating and slab building.

**1** Deposit the clay between the two roller guides and begin to scree the slop with a straight edge.

**2** Continue until the surface of the slop is completely smooth.

If you are planning to print texture into a slab (with or without fibre clay), do so while the slab is soft and flat on a work surface.

**3** When the slab is firm enough to peel away from the plaster, lift it away for immediate use or wrap it in plastic for later use.

The advantage of using fibre clay slabs is that they are particularly strong when working with thin structures. They are also flexible to bend and mend easily if broken or cracked (see fibrous and paper clay).

## Bringing flat slabs to leatherhard

All rolled or harp cut slabs will curl at the edges unless they are dried slowly and weighted with flat boards. Place one or two sheets of newspaper on the top and bottom faces of each slab to prevent them sticking to the board. The newspaper will also absorb moisture from the slabs and help bring them to the required firmness. If you do not have enough boards, interface the slabs with newspaper and stack them two to three high and weight them down. Put any larger slabs under smaller ones so they all remain flat. Slabs and boards can be interspersed in a stack. Check the slabs periodically to make sure they are not getting too dry. As soon as they can stand on their edge like cardboard without buckling, they are ready. Leatherhard slabs should be made at least a day in advance to allow them to firm up sufficiently.

It is vital to keep slabs at this leatherhard stage until your joining work is complete, so remove the boards and cover the entire stack with plastic to keep it airtight and prevent further drying. Weight the stack with a board at the top and leave it overnight so that it evens out to a consistent firmness.

TWO LIPPED VASES
(21 CM/8¼ IN AND 31 CM/12 IN)
WHITE EARTHENWARE LEATHERHARD SLABS ARE ROLLED OUT BY HAND, CUT OUT, SCORED AND JOINED. THE PIECES ARE DECORATED WITH COLOURED SLIPS USING SGRAFFITO AND RESIST TECHNIQUES. FINALLY THE PIECES ARE BURNISHED, BISCUIT (BISQUE) FIRED, GLAZED INSIDE AND FIRED AGAIN (LIZ BECKENHAM).

## Soft slabbing

Unlike leatherhard slabs, soft slabs should be made as you need them. The degree of flaccidity required will depend on the slab's height, its plasticity, extremity of curve and the angle at which it is to be placed. The only way to gauge the correct flaccidity of a soft slab is through trial and error.

To keep soft slab work alive and fresh it is best to approach it with the minimum amount of handling possible. The more you touch the slabs, the more tired their appearance will become. Wait until the work has firmed up and become leatherhard before you do any cleaning or trimming. Likewise, to retain the

tautness to a piece, any further alterations should be made when the work is able to support the pressure and weight of more clay. This rule also applies when treating the final stages of the top edge or rim of a piece.

When soft slabs are very wet they can be pressed together with little more than a damp sponge or by pinching or pressing an overlap. The resulting seams can be left untouched to show the workings of the joining process. Edges and planes can be treated in many ways – squeezed and pinched, pushed and eased, manipulated and bellied, cut and pierced, gouged and rolled or dropped from a height to take on the feel of billowing fabric.

'FROM A DREAM', USING LEATHERHARD SLABS (KARI CHRISTENSEN).

## Using soft slabs

Soft slabs can be wrapped around straight sided formers, such as cardboard tubes or shaped blocks of wood. This is a fast method suitable for making cylinders or other shapes that can be distorted to other shapes, such as ovals or squares, before attaching them to a base or leaving them to become firm. Once leatherhard, you can also use the formed shapes as components and you can make further additions.

**1** Cover the former tightly with a sheet of newspaper and secure it with sticky tape. Wrap the slab around the former. To make a chamfered join, place the edge of the slab to be cut so it overhangs the bench edge. Hold a knife tip at an angle and run it through the overlapping slab. Remove the excess piece before preparing the edges for joining.

**2** Join the wrapped shape to its base while it is still on its former, but remove the former before the clay firms and shrinks onto it. The newspaper around the former will help it slide out of the shape without sticking to the soft clay. Finally, cut away the excess clay of the base and pare and clean the shape. Final cleaning up to the piece can be done at the leatherhard stage.

STANDING FORM (39 CM/15½ IN)
USING SLABS BETWEEN SOFT AND
LEATHERHARD, THE SLABS STAND
ALONE, BUT WILL ALSO CURVE
(ALISON BRITTON).
PHOTOGRAPH BY DAVID CRIPPS.

## Using slurry for joining slabs

This technique is used for all types of slab building and for any joining process with clay – it is used when joining soft clay to leatherhard, leatherhard to leatherhard, and soft or leatherhard slabs to bone dry fibrous clay. Ensure that you are familiar with this process before embarking on any of the projects or starting any work in clay.

Start the joining process by making the slurry, which must match the clay you are using. Cover small, bone dry pieces of clay with water. Allow the clay to dissolve before stirring to a consistency between single (light) and double (heavy) cream. Make an ample supply of slurry and store it in an airtight container.

Apply the slurry to the faces of each piece to be joined using a stiff brush or toothbrush. Next, thoroughly score the slurried faces using the tip of a pointed knife. Push the two pieces together giving them a slight wiggle as you do so until the scored surfaces knot together.

Remove any excess slurry emerging from the join using a damp sponge, tool or kidney before it dries. No matter how small the pieces are, clay must be joined using this method to make an effective bond that will not pull apart during drying and firing. Let the work become firm before giving the slurried seams a final trim and cleaning them up. This will give a cleaner finish to the work.

### Joining fibre clay

When attaching a slab to bone dry fibrous clay, the fibrous clay face should be soaked with water before slurrying and scoring (see above).

### Cutting out

Trim the slab to size and get rid of any dry edges to ensure the work will join firmly and will not pull apart when drying. Allow extra length for an overlap if butt joining (see above), which can be trimmed and cleaned up later. This gives a cleaner finish to flat work. Before making a final cut to a slab to be joined, check its fit by holding where it is to be placed. Mark where the cuts should be with the tip of a knife.

**1** When making a butted join allow an extra length for an overlap which can be trimmed and cleaned up at the leatherhard stage.

**2** Trim and straighten a butted join or corner once leatherhard by running a metal kidney along a metal ruler, slightly inset to the edge.

**3** When joining slabs end to end follow the same process, apply slurry, score the edge faces and push them to knot together.

**4** Slabs can also be overlapped when joined. When joining slabs to a flat base, stand the walls on the top of the base, rather than on its sides. This will pull the walls in and prevent the work pulling apart at the seams.

- When joining clay slabs or other forms, the internal face can be reinforced by applying a soft coil of clay along the internal corner and smoothing it back with a tool. If the join is thorough, this added labour is not always necessary.

- To trim the base edge of the joined slabs when the piece is leatherhard, drag the work to overhang the surface on which it is sitting to get a clear line of attack with the hacksaw blade, kidney or any other tools.

**5** Making a chamfered cut to a slab will allow it to sit at an angle. The degree of the chamfer will dictate the slant of the wall.

# TECHNIQUES
# EXTRUSION The principle of extruding clay extends from the idea of a wad box (extruder) that

is used for making wads, or snakes, of clay for setting saggars. The extruded strips of clay can be varied

in profile by using interchangeable dies that fit into the wad box (see Equipment, handbuilding).

■ Wad boxes or extruders can be used for making strips in various shapes and sizes suitable for coiling. Narrow sheets can be produced for slab building, which combined with an open clay will not warp and can be cut to form tiles or test pieces for glaze tests. You can also use it to make handles for repeat pieces or domestic ware. Dies can be cut to suit the scale or design of the piece.

Soft strips can be altered, curved and waved, and then left to firm before fixing into place. The extruded clay lengths can be given a fluid or rigid feel as required. Left to become leatherhard they can be cut cleanly without leaving finger marks. Straight, long extruded strips should be turned frequently while drying as they are prone to curling and warping. Hollow extrusions can be used as components of an assembled piece or to form containers by attachment to a base.

### Joining
Use the usual slurry and score method to join extruded strips of clay or hollow shapes at the leatherhard stage (see using slurry for joining slabs). Joins to cut sections or components can be filled with soft clay once the work has firmed to leatherhard to clean up any gaps. Wipe away marks or excess joining slurry with a damp sponge.

## Preparing clay for extrusion

An extruder or wad box is used to extrude clay strips by forcing them through a die (see examples of dies shown in Equipment, handbuilding). Make a rolled, flat-ended sausage to fit inside the collar of the extruder. The clay should be soft enough to push through the extruder with ease.

## Extruding shapes

Hollow sections of any shape can be extruded using a die with a fixed inner plate. Their thickness is dependent on the space between the inner and outer plates of the die. Cut into pieces, the extruded shapes can be treated as components to be joined when leatherhard or to make complicated or simple, functional or sculptural structures.

If you don't have access to a wad box, you can use a hooped wire (trimming) tool or shaped hoop of wire. Pull the hooped tool through a prepared, soft block of clay and ease the clay apart to remove the clay strip.

A clay gun is a useful alternative for making smaller decorative extrusions that can be applied to work as raised relief. Soft extrusions will join to plastic clay with slurry alone and a little pressure applied with a damp sponge. Allow the work to dry slowly to prevent extruded pieces falling away from the surface.

Small coils made with a clay gun can be arranged as a "drawn" line and attached or rolled into a slab of clay while both are soft. Use compatible clays that have a close shrinkage rate.

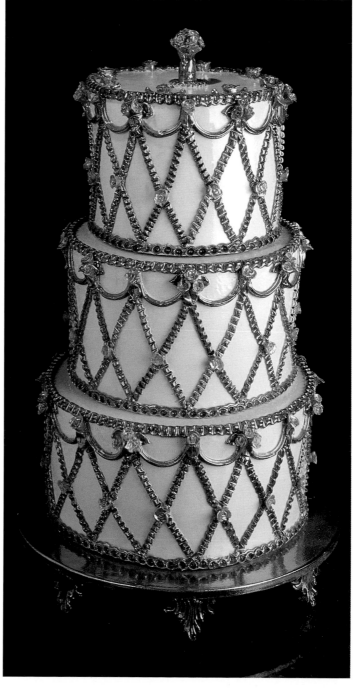

St Bride's Tower (60 cm/24 in)
Slab built and decorated with extruded coils that
are then indented with a modelling tool at
regular intervals to create a convoluted edge
(Rachel Kneebone).

# TECHNIQUES
# CLAY RELIEF

Small, soft pieces of clay can be built up in stages onto firmed previous applications of clay until the required height or shape is achieved. Modelled clay can be integrated or joined on to clay formed by any of the handbuilding techniques using the score and slurry technique wherever the surface is leatherhard. When joining soft clay to soft, however, a gentle pressure to smear on the clay is usually sufficient. Leave any final carving of the modelled clay until the built-up clay is leatherhard to achieve a crisp finish.

■ Clay bas-relief that is thicker than 2 cm (¾ in) must be hollowed out from the back to reduce the thickness of the wall for drying and firing. This enables water in the clay to escape as the work is heated in the kiln and prevent it from exploding with the pressure of evaporating water or steam. Thick forms should be fired slowly in the initial stages until the kiln has reached red heat or 600ºC (1112ºF).

### Modelling

All solid, modelled forms should be scooped out from the inside and emptied. Use a hooped wire trimming tool and leave a wall thick enough to support the modelled clay outer structure. Solid figures can be cut with a knife, hollowed and rejoined by slurrying and scoring (see using slurry for joining slabs) while they are still leatherhard. This allows access to a solid area that cannot be reached from a base opening, such as for a head or the upper body sections of a figure.

When hollowing out a thick wall, use a hooped wire (trimming) tool to scoop out a little at a time when the work is firm enough to hold and turn without damage. Rest the overturned work on a pad or sponge to protect the front face.

### Applying bas-relief

Small pieces of clay can be built up following the usual rules of joining to leatherhard clay (see using slurry for joining slabs). Soft clay can be joined to soft with applied pressure using fingers or tools. Modelled surfaces built up in this way can be applied to any angle or area of clay made by any forming method, as long as there is sufficient strength to support the weight of the applied clay and the pressure of the tools.

COCKEREL TUREEN WITH TAIL FEATHER
LADLE (35 CM/14 IN)
WHITE EARTHENWARE AND C-MATERIAL,
COILED, SCRAPED AND MODELLED WITH
BASE COILED ONTO A CURVED SLAB. ALL
DETAILS HAVE BEEN MODELLED BY
BUILDING UP SMALL PIECES OF CLAY
(ANNA LAMBERT).

# TECHNIQUES
# DECORATING INTO CLAY

Clay is a wonderful material for picking up texture and can be treated in a number of ways to achieve a range of textural qualities and surfaces. There are many techniques to create raised and applied texture or to decorate into clay. When working into clay, the wall or slab must be thick enough to manage the depth of the imprint or tool. Separately worked pieces of clay can be fixed onto a surface with the slurry and score method (see using slurry for joining slabs).

## Indenting

Indenting techniques involve making a mark into clay with a tool, such as a stamp, roulette or carving tool. These raised clay surfaces look effective with colour washes which pick out the raised textures, glazes that break at high points or coloured transparent glazes that collect in the indented areas making rich tones.

Clay can be carved in the same way as wood, using any tool that gives the required effect. For a crisp, hard edge carve clay when it is leatherhard. The softer the clay, the softer the finish will be. The tool you use and the state of the clay will dictate the quality of the carved edge. Carve into a thick-walled flat surface or a raised relief area to produce a sharp-edged sculpted feel.

Pieces of foam sheet, card (cardboard) or plastic sheet can be cut and rolled into soft clay to give a variety of edges and depths to the impressed shape. This is a useful technique for impressing letters or numbers into clay. You can also cut out shapes when they are firm and apply them to a formed clay surface.

Detailed textures can be picked up on soft clay, which is laid flat, or by impressing stamps into built or thrown walls still soft enough to imprint. You can also attach individual pieces of stamped clay to a wall.

Stamps can be made by carving plaster (see Making and Using Moulds) or clay, which is fired before use. Roulettes can be carved in plaster, clay and wood or improvised using items such as cogs or bottle tops. Unlike stamps, they make a continuous, patterned circuit, which can be applied quickly to a soft piece of work. Strips of rouletted clay can also be cut and attached to a piece of work.

TRAYS
SLAB BUILT WITH IMPRESSED
TEXTURE, HIGH FIRED STONEWARE
WITH THIN SHINO GLAZE (TAVS
JORGENSEN).

## Inlaying

When indented areas or lines of clay are filled with a contrasting coloured clay or thick slip, this is known as inlaying. The inlaid clay or slip is scraped back level with the surrounding clay once it is leatherhard.

EGG (18 CM/7 IN)
SLIP CAST FORM, INLAID
AND COLOURED (JANE WALLER).

**1** Allow the surface to be inlaid to become leatherhard. Indented areas can be inlaid with a contrasting soft clay or a thick, yogurt consistency slip applied with a brush. Fill the inlay so it is proud of the height of the impressed areas for both methods if you require a final level surface. If using clay slip, build it up in successive layers after each has first become dry to the touch. If using a contrasting coloured clay, select one with a similar shrinkage rate to the main clay.

**2** Ensure the clay is at the dry end of the scale of leatherhard to prevent any contrasting colours in the inlay from blurring. For a clean, level finish scrape back the inlaid clay or slip using the edge of a metal kidney until it is level with its surrounding surface. Allow the work to dry slowly to prevent the inlaid clay from cracking.

## Sprigging

Sprigs are made by pushing soft clay into a plaster mould (see Lady Daisy Jug project), then levelling with a wire harp or plastic card.

**1** The dry, plaster mould absorbs moisture and makes the sprigs shrink so they come out of the mould easily. Remove the sprigs with a needle, by tapping them out or lifting them out with a piece of soft clay.

**2** Slurry the sprig's attaching face while supporting it in your other hand with a piece of clay before joining it to the surface you are decorating. Thicker sprigs should be slurried and scored, as should the attaching surface. Use an appropriate tool to clarify any details and remove excess slurry. Work should be dried slowly, particularly if you have used fine sprigs that could not be scored before attachment.

EARTHENWARE VESSEL (10 CM/4 IN)
SPRIGGED DECORATION, THICK, HIGH SHRINKAGE SLIPS
APPLIED AND IRON AND CHROME GLAZED IN AN
OXIDIZING ATMOSPHERE (ASHLEY HOWARD).

## Fluting and faceting

The technique of fluting involves cutting a series of parallel, concave grooves into clay using a round-ended tool. This traditionally wheel-based technique gives a controlled, carved, gouged pattern to a clay wall. Faceting, on the other hand, involves making regularly spaced and sized flat cuts to a clay wall using a straight-edged tool, such as a cutting harp (U-shaped rod) or knife. This technique results in a carved or chiselled pattern. These methods are particularly dramatic when combined with glazes that break at the high points of the cuts, such as a black tenmoku glaze that breaks to orange or tan. This method can also be used in a less rigid manner to create fluid or assymmetrical forms.

BOTTLES AND LIDDED
FORMS (20–35 CM/8–14 IN)
KEUPER RED STONEWARE CLAY
(OCHRE), AND EARTHENWARE
CLAY (PURPLE). BOTTLES ARE
THROWN AND FLUTED
(EMILY MYERS).

To cut flutes into a clay wall, measure and mark out the point at which the cut starts and ends to ensure the circuit will meet. If you require a clean, hard edge, ensure the clay wall is leatherhard. Fluting appears to be a simple technique, but it requires a trained hand and eye to cut each flute evenly to the right depth and alignment. Flutes can be cut at any angle running parallel or at an angle, as shown here.

Faceting, like fluting, involves marking out where each cut will run from and to, as well as the width of each cut. The fewer cuts made around the piece, the thicker the wall needs to be. For clean, hard-edged cuts, and to avoid a thin wall collapsing, facet the wall when it is leatherhard.

## Piercing

This technique can be used to cut, pierce or prick a formal, complicated or loose pattern of holes into a clay wall. The holes can be made into leatherhard clay for a clean effect; loose, free piercing into soft clay will add movement to a wall.

Plan and mark complicated, lattice style piercing before cutting and wait until the clay is leatherhard for clean cuts.

## Wiping back, scraping and compressing

To alter the finished surface of plastic or leatherhard clay, the top layer can be roughened or smoothed by wiping back, scraping or compressing. These techniques can be used and combined to build up decorative surfaces. They can either be applied to a clay slab before it is formed, or to a form that has already been thrown, moulded, or handbuilt.

**1** Prepare the slab or form your piece.

**2** Place a piece of newspaper or paint wax resist in the shape of your chosen decoration on the surface of the clay. Allow any wax resist to dry.

**3** Sponge clay away from areas around the resist. The resist will leave a raised area of clay with a soft edge.

Scraping with a metal kidney or sponging with a damp sponge on open or sandy clay will drag or reveal sand on the surface giving a rough texture. Conversely, smoothing pressure with the edge of a metal or plastic kidney will compress the clay to give a smooth texture. You can use surface scraping, smoothing and wiping back to make contrasting textures of clay – the result will be affected by the nature of the clay you have used.

## Burnishing

A smooth object, such as the back of a spoon or a smooth pebble, can be used to burnish the surface of leatherhard clay. Most clays are suitable for burnishing, although finer clay gives a smoother surface. A greater shine will be achieved when the clay surface is on the firm side of leatherhard. Clay painted with decorating slips can also be burnished. Terra sigillata, a fine particled, siliceous slip, gives an extremely smooth burnished finish.

Move the burnishing tool in circular or linear strokes. Once dry, fire the burnished piece at 950–1080°C (1742–1976°F) to retain the shine. Finally apply the burnished areas with a clear wax or neutral shoe polish to enhance the colour and seal the surface.

## Combining coloured clays (millefiori)

The random or controlled combining of coloured clays is known as millefiori. The name derives from a Roman glass making technique using brightly coloured discs of glass, fused together to make a sheet.

The white clays here were stained by kneading in colour additions (see preparing clay) and then rolled together in layers. Strips of coloured clay have also been sandwiched in layers that have been sliced while the clay was still plastic.

Place the coloured pieces together in a hollow plaster mould while still soft and cover them with thin plastic. Pound them together using a pestle. Leave the work to become leatherhard, close to dry, and then scrape the surface with a metal kidney to give a smooth finish.

Different coloured clays with closely matched shrinkage rates can also be combined. Such work must be dried slowly by wrapping loosely in plastic to extend the drying time. This prevents the coloured areas separating, appearing as cracks on seams between adjacent colours. Work should be covered with a glaze that will react with or reveal the coloured clays on firing.

## Marbling or agate work

Contrasting clays used for marbled or agate work are loosely combined at the clay preparation stage (see preparing clay). The combined clays should have the same or similar shrinkage rates.

To obtain a dramatic marbled effect the proportion of lighter clay should exceed that of the darker clay. Agate is a stone that displays multicoloured layers when sliced, hence the term agateware.

Combined clays can be used with any handbuilding technique. The clay is scraped back at the firm to dry leatherhard stage to reveal clean areas of coloured clay. Work made using marbled clays should be covered with a glaze suitable for reacting with the coloured clays on firing, or a transparent glaze to reveal them.

## Using Egyptian paste

This is essentially a clay body that has the glaze ingredients contained within the clay, Egyptian paste lacks plasticity and is difficult to handle. It is therefore best worked by moulding, carving and piercing; the glaze colour will reveal itself when the clay is fired.

It is important to ensure that glaze never comes into contact with kiln furniture as it will stick fast. Because anything made from Egyptian paste cannot be placed directly on a kiln shelf, they need to be suspended. Beads, for example, should be fired on Nichrome wire racks.

### Shiny Egyptian paste recipe

It is not easy to buy Egyptian paste ready made, so you will need to have a reliable recipe to follow. Here is one of the many tried and tested ones. You will also need weighing scales, a face mask (respirator), protective gloves and an old washing-up bowl. Use cone orton 06–04 (see Glazing and Firing, firing times and temperatures).

### Ingredients

BASE
800 g (1 lb 12 oz) Potash feldspar
400 g (14 oz) Flint
500 g (17½ oz) China clay
100 g (3½ oz) Ball clay
120 g (4¼ oz) Sodium bicarbonate
120 g (4¼ oz) Soda ash
100 g (3½ oz) Whiting
160 g (5⅝ oz) Fine white sand

COLOUR ADDITIONS
For a green paste:
  3% chrome
For a turquoise paste:
  3% black copper oxide
For a blue paste:
  1–3% cobalt carbonate
For a black paste:
  3% manganese dioxide
For a brown paste:
  3% red iron oxide

### Method

**1** For the base mixture weigh each dry ingredient and place them in the bowl.

**2** Add a little water at a time until there is enough to make a doughy mixture similar to the consistency of plastic clay.

**3** Remove the base mixture and knead it on a flat surface until all the ingredients are thoroughly combined.

**4** Add the required percentage of colour addition to the dry ingredients in the bowl or knead it into the base.

AZTEC BOWL (12 CM/4½ IN)
WHITE EARTHENWARE CLAY STAINED WITH
NATURAL OXIDES AND BLACK BODY STAIN. EACH
SHAPE IS BEATEN INTO A SPECIALLY MADE PLANTER
MOULD AND THE PIECES ARE PESTLED TOGETHER.
THE MILLEFIORI PATTERNING IS SCRAPED CLEAR
AFTER THE PIECE HAS DRIED TO LEATHERHARD
(JANE WALLER).

# MAKING AND USING MOULDS

**MOULDS CAN BE USED IN MANY WAYS** IN CERAMICS – FOR PRODUCING REPEAT FORMS, FOR MAKING COMPONENTS THAT CAN THEN BE ASSEMBLED, FOR CREATING SHAPED BASES OR STARTING POINTS FROM WHICH A PIECE CAN BEGIN, OR FOR APPLYING TEXTURE AND DECORATION. MOULDS RANGE FROM SIMPLE DROP OUT MOULDS TO MORE COMPLEX PIECE MOULDS. READY-MADE MOULDS ARE AVAILABLE TO BUY, BUT THE ADVANTAGE OF MAKING YOUR OWN IS THAT IT IS POSSIBLE TO TAILOR THE MOULD TO YOUR DESIGN, COMBINING AN INDUSTRIAL PROCESS WITH A PERSONAL CHARACTER AND STYLE.

# TECHNIQUES

## PLASTER A naturally occurring gypsum, plaster was first mined for commercial ceramic purposes in Montmartre, Paris in the 1770s, hence the name "plaster of Paris". It is made by a calcination process of crushing, grinding and heating the gypsum to remove chemically bound water.

▨ Plaster is crucial for the production of commercial ceramics. It is also invaluable for the individual craftsperson producing highly original work.

When plaster is mixed with water to produce a pourable mix, the water lost in the calcination processes is taken up again to form a solid, set mass. Excess water is dried off leaving numerous minute pores that give moulds their essential porous quality.

Abundant, and inexpensive, there are many types of plaster. Among the most widely used are Pottery plaster or Newcast plaster for mouldmaking, and Crystacal R and Keramicast plaster for modelmaking. Avoid buying more plaster than you can use within a few weeks. It is difficult to keep plaster for long periods, unless it is in a completely airtight container.

## Mixing and pouring plaster

For most ceramic purposes, you can achieve a good, average water-to-plaster ratio visually without any weighing. Remember that the higher the water to plaster ratio, the weaker the set plaster will be.

Measuring plaster to water proportions by weight rather than volume is recommended when greater casting precision is required. For example, piece moulds for slip casting require each section of the mould to be consistently porous. This is achieved by accurately weighing and measuring the water-to-plaster ratios. The various Newcast plasters vary in both wear strength and surface finish. All plasters will become hot and expand slightly as they set.

### TYPICAL PLASTER-TO-WATER PROPORTIONS
The best results with plaster are achieved when plaster and water are accurately measured.

|  | POTTERY (moulds) | NEWCAST 71/80 (moulds & fine detail) | NEWCAST 96 (moulds) | KERAMICAST (modelmaking) | CRYSTACAL R (modelmaking) |
|---|---|---|---|---|---|
| PLASTER | 1.4 kg (3¼ lb) | 1.3 kg (3¾ lb) | 1.4 kg (3¼ lb) | 1.5 kg (3¼ lb) | 2.8 kg (7 lb) |
| WATER | 1 litre (1¾ pints) | 1 litre (1¾ pints) | 1 litre (1¾ pints) | 1 litre (1¾ pints) | 1 litre (1¾ pints) |

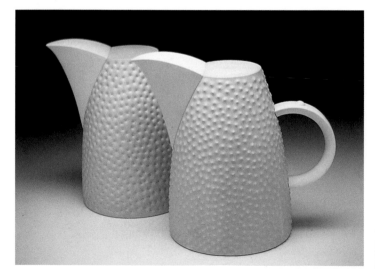

TEXTURED JUGS
(24 CM/9½ IN), MADE WITH
PLASTER MODELS (TAVS
JORGENSEN).

**1** To work out proportions visually, look at the area to be filled and estimate the volume of water it will take. Pour it into a plastic container. Add a little extra water just in case as plaster for a mould or slab should be poured in one batch. Gradually sift or strew in the plaster until it breaks in small peaks through the surface of the water. Always add plaster to water, never the other way round.

Leave the plaster undisturbed to soak up water for 1–2 minutes and then stir. Be careful not to pull in air by breaking the surface. Use one hand to stir, keeping the other plaster-free. Periodically remove air bubble scum from the surface with a rubber kidney. Continue stirring until the plaster begins to feel heavy. It is now ready to pour.

**NB** NEVER WASH LARGE AMOUNTS OF PLASTER DOWN THE SINK BECAUSE IT CAN BLOCK YOUR PLUMBING. A SETTLING TANK (SINK TRAP) WILL ENABLE YOU TO WASH SMALL AMOUNTS OF PLASTER DOWN THE SINK (SEE WORKSHOP LAYOUT).

**2** Pour the plaster immediately in a thin continuous stream against the inner side of the cottle (see Equipment, mouldmaking), again to prevent air being pulled into the cast causing bubbles on the surface of a model or weaknesses in the plaster.

Before the plaster has set, give sharp successive taps to the supporting board under the cast until air bubbles no longer rise to the surface of the poured plaster. While the plaster is still wet, remove any excess using a rubber kidney. Wash any residue off your hand and the container immediately before it sets.

**3** Once the plaster is set and has been released from the model and/or the retaining wall, file away sharp corners of the cast mould using a surform blade then allow it to dry before use.

Plaster casts should be dried to a maximum of 60°C (140°F) and removed from the heat as soon as they are dry. They will deteriorate rapidly if they are dried at too high a temperature.

Store your plaster and made casts in a very dry place. If they absorb moisture the setting time of plaster will shorten and they will lose strength.

LARGE BOWLS (14 CM/5½ IN)
WHITE EARTHENWARE CLAY,
COLOURED SLIP, TRANSPARENT
GLAZE, JIGGER AND JOLLEY
PRODUCTION METHOD
(JULIE GOODWIN).

# TECHNIQUES
# MOULDMAKING
Using one shape of mould can be repetitive and limiting, but if moulds are used for assembling components or as a starting point for work this does not have to be the case. Many makers who concentrate on the decorated finish rather than the making process choose to use moulds as an efficient, commercial option.

## Making moulds and models

Solid models for slip casting, press moulding and sprig moulds are made either using plaster or clay.

Circular shaped models can either be turned from plaster on a lathe, or plaster can be shaped with a profile former or a model thrown in clay as a solid shape on the wheel.

Whether to use plaster or clay depends on the form to be cast and the quality and precision required. Other shapes can be sledged in clay (see hollow and hump moulds) or hand modelled in clay. Producing a model in clay involves fewer steps, though it can also be used in conjunction with the waste mould technique as a starting point for developing a clay model into a plaster one.

Plaster models have advantages over clay in that they do not distort during casting, their surfaces can be sanded with wet and dry carborundum paper (wet and dry sandpaper) to a smooth surface and any breakages can be repaired with polystyrene (rubber) cement or strong glue. Found objects such as pebbles, shells and screws can be used as models from which to make moulds. Plaster casts can also be taken of such objects.

Indents and scratches on clay models can be filled by smoothing in soft clay. Those on plaster models can be temporarily fixed with clay or, if deep, filled with plaster and smoothed down once the plaster has set.

FIG. 1

model

Undercuts in plaster moulds are caused by indents, small scratches or changes in direction in a model, particularly one made in plaster. The plaster sets around an undercut shape therefore "locking it" into the plaster (see Fig. 1). In this case it would not be possible to remove this model from the mould without breaking it. This does not necessarily restrict the design of the model from which you are making a mould (the problem in Fig. 1 can be overcome by using the three-piece mould in Fig. 2). However, adapting a design might make the mould-making process a less complex one, so always consider the practical application of your mould as soon as you start designing.

FIG. 2

model

A piece mould (a mould made up of pieces) allows you to plan for undercuts and changes in direction (see Fig. 2). The three pieces are dismantled to release the model.

FIG. 3

adapted model

When plaster is cast over a model to produce a mould, the plaster will expand outward away from the surface of the model. When casting a hump mould, for example, plaster is cast into a negative to make a positive shape, the expansion is directed towards the walls of the mould. Therefore each wall of the mould, except the top one, must be tapered, known as 'draft', allowing the positive mould to be withdrawn easily from the negative model (see Fig. 3).

## Using seam, or parting, lines

**1** If your model is asymmetrical and, because of undercuts, cannot be split in a straight line to create two halves, you need to set up the point where the mould divides, known as the seam, or parting, line. The line is first marked out on the model with an indelible pencil if the model is made from plaster or by scoring if the model is clay. Rest the model on clay supports and use an end face as a guide to rest the model at 90° to its base.

**2** The clay is then built up around the model, to the marked parting line drawn on the model. Doing this blocks off the areas that will be cast at a later stage. The built up clay is modelled to a smooth surface.

The irregular design of the vases above involved establishing the seam line before casting the mould in three pieces: one for each side of the vase and the third mould for the base.

GRAIN TEMPLE 11 (23 × 15 × 30 CM/9 × 6 × 12 IN) CERAMIC, TERRA SIGILLATA, STAINS, OXIDES (JANET WILLIAMS).

### Running plaster and facing up

When running (pouring) plaster onto another piece of plaster, you must apply the separating agent "soft soap" in a process that is known as "facing up" ("sizing"). It is essential that any plaster piece to be cast is wet before being faced up (sized), so it needs to be soaked in water for at least 10–15 minutes unless it has been freshly cast, in which case it will still be wet.

Facing up (sizing) must be done thoroughly. The agent (size) should be applied to boards, table surfaces and cottling walls – in fact to any surface that is likely to come in contact with the poured plaster, particularly if it is made of a porous material. The soft soap should be dissolved from its jelly-like state into a liquid consistency using warm water before being applied to any of the surfaces.

Other releasing agents that are sometimes used are petroleum jelly when casting body parts or various oils when soft soap is not available.

Apply liquid soap with a natural sponge and allow it to soak into the plaster for about 15 seconds. Remove any excess suds with a second wet-to-damp natural sponge, rinsing it out with water when necessary. Repeat the two soaping and wiping actions using the different sponges until a gloss appears on the plaster surface. This can take up to 12 applications. No suds or water droplets should remain – use a paint brush to clean any crevices and difficult spots. Any further handling of the soaped (sized) model or mould should be avoided until after the plaster has been poured.

### Preparing to pour plaster

Before mixing or pouring plaster over a model you need to set up a wall or dam of stiff material, called a cottle, framing board or side set to form the sides of the cast. Cast plaster bats or smooth wood can be used for straight side sets; thick, flexible plastic or sheet metal is normally used for curved walls.

For total accuracy, plaster bats are cast on a sheet of glass and scored or sawn to the correct size when they are set. Remember, plaster side sets must be faced up (sized) before they come into contact with poured plaster.

### Fixing a cottle

Fix a cottle with strong tape to reinforce it and prevent the cottle from being forced outwards with the weight of the plaster.

The cottle must also be secured to prevent any leaks. You can use clay coils to help secure the retaining wall. Straight-sided walls can be secured with a builder's strap or tightened string secured around the outside of the retaining wall.

Make a final check by holding the wall or walls and testing them for any play or weakness, particularly for any shapes that require a great volume of plaster. If you are using a clay model, ensure it has not been damaged by the cottle.

Any clay used for cottling, as with any clay contaminated with plaster, should be either thrown away or stored separately from clean clay. This should be reused solely for plaster making purposes.

Take into account the fact that any cottle must be solidly secured in to place about 3–5 cm (1½–2 in) from the edge of the model and ensure that the supporting board or base set allows room for this gap (see below). The base set is the flat, smooth and level board on which the model sits. It should be 1–2 cm (½–¾ in) thick to provide a guide against which to rest the base edge of the cottle wall at 90° to the board. The base set will ultimately provide a neater finish to your cast shape, as well as greater accuracy, which is an essential requirement for making piece moulds.

### Making a plaster bat

When making side sets (retaining walls), plaster bats or clay reclaiming bats (see preparing clay), you do not need to spend time planning as there is no model to take into consideration.

In this case plaster can be poured directly on to a smooth flat surface, such as formica, marble or glass, inside a secured cottle wall. Four wooden bats are used to form a square cottle, secured with a brick on each corner.

When making plaster bats for reclaiming clay, they should be of a greater thickness than printing or side set bats. Make a higher cottle wall from wooden boards, securing them with clay or string. This gives added strength for the extra plaster when casting.

# TECHNIQUES
# HOLLOW AND HUMP MOULDS These moulds, also called press moulds, are

used for press-moulding shapes. You can buy ready-made moulds for press moulds but the disadvantage

of this is that you are limited by a set design. The technique that follows explains how to make your own.

**1** To form a clay model for a dish or hollow mould, sledge a profile around a clay body using a profile former made of metal or wood. Pull the notched former along the edge of the base set, which will act as a guide to shape the soft clay.

**2** Position a faced up (sized) (see running plaster and facing up), supported side set (retaining wall) around the base set and model and fix it in place. Carefully pour the plaster inside the supported walls covering the clay model to a depth of approximately 3 cm (1 in). Leave the plaster to set for 15–30 minutes and then remove the side set (retaining wall). Gouge away the clay model with a wooden tool to reveal the plaster mould. Clean up the freshly made hollow mould with a surform blade.

**3** Face up (size) the hollow mould before positioning and securing the side set (retaining wall) around it. Ensure the side set (retaining wall) is positioned to allow for the height of plaster that is to be poured into the hollow mould to make the hump mould.

BLACK BOWL (24 CM/9½ IN)
CRANK CLAY, PRESS MOULDED
AND SLAB BUILT, INLAID
COLOUR AND STAINED BODY
(PHILIP JOLLEY).

**4** When the cast of the hump, or drape, mould is set, hold a metal disc against the plaster cast and apply firm, muted taps with a rubber mallet. Repeat the taps around the sides of the cast to send dispersed shock blows through the plaster parts until you detect movement of the parting line or until the tone of the tap changes. This will indicate that the plaster is going to release. Ease the positive and negative casts apart. Pouring water onto the parting line can also help to release the plaster parts.

# TECHNIQUES
## PRESS MOULDING
Press moulding with plaster moulds achieves identical shapes in large quantities with relative ease. The pressed shapes can be used as a base on which to coil, slab build or otherwise extend the work. The rims of pressed shapes can be cut or adjoined with handles or decorative applied relief. Press moulds are used for millefiori and hump moulds and enable inlaid or textured decoration to be pressed out without interfering with the upper face of the pressing.

### Press-moulding hollow moulds

Symmetrical clay shapes can be made as a pair and joined together while leatherhard to make an enclosed form. Assymetrical shapes such as handles, teapot spouts, figurines and pots can also be press moulded in two halves that are then joined.

**1** Lie a rolled, soft slab of clay over the hollow mould using a cloth to hold onto the clay.

**2** Ease the slab into place using a damp sponge to prevent your fingers indenting the soft clay. Any folds in the clay slab can be smoothed away using the curve of first a serrated and then a smooth metal kidney. Use a flexible rubber kidney to make a final finish.

**3** Trim the edges level with the mould. Do any final shaping, trimming and cleaning when the clay is leatherhard and it can be removed without distorting. Rounded bases can be tapped flat on a surface while the shape is firm, but soft enough to give.

### Draping over a hump mould

Slabs of clay that are printed, inlaid or textured while they lie flat on a work surface, are ideal for using with the draped working method. A coiled or separately moulded footring (rim) can be joined to the shape, often an open dish, while it is resting on the hump mould.

**1** Inlaid or textured slabs can be draped over a hump mould (drape mould) and pressed in place without interfering with the inlaid or textured face. Ease the slab into place using a damp sponge and rubber kidney.

**2** Trim back edges with a cutting harp (wire), either level to the mould's edge or with an overhang as required. Further shaping and cleaning of the edges can be done when the shape has firmed and been removed from the mould.

**3** To prevent the shape cracking as it shrinks onto the mould, remove draped shapes before they become too dry.

# TECHNIQUES
# JIGGER AND JOLLEY The technique of jigger and jolley involves the use of accurately

made and centered plaster moulds placed and held by a cup wheel head, which revolves like a thrower's wheel. Jiggering is an efficient method of producing quantities of bowls and plates – most commercial dinnerware is manufactured in this way.

■ The plaster mould in jiggering forms the inside shape of plates and other flatware, while in jollying it forms the outside shape of open cups and bowls.

A pivoted, counter-balanced arm holding a fixed metal profile is brought down onto the clay. The profile then spreads the clay onto the mould in an even section. Excess clay spread along to the rim of the mould is then trimmed with a knife and the arm is brought down again to contact the clay with the profile giving the clay its final shape.

Many working moulds can be cast from the master models which are usually turned using a lathe or whirler (banding wheel). As with other plaster mould techniques, large numbers of working moulds may be necessary as work cannot be removed from the mould until it is leatherhard.

The picture above shows the jigger and jolley process used with a pre-decorated slip tailored and laid into the mould, finished off with the revolving template.

PLATE (24 CM/9½ IN)
WHITE EARTHENWARE
CLAY, COLOURED
CLAY INLAYS AND
TRANSPARENT GLAZE
(SABINA TEUTEBERG).

COFFECUP SAUCERS
JOLLEYED, HIGH FIRED
STONEWARE WITH BARIUM
GREEN GLAZE, DESIGNED
FOR THE ROYAL CRESCENT
HOTEL, BATH, ENGLAND
(TAVS JORGENSEN).

# TECHNIQUES
# SLIP CASTING
Suitable for making large volumes of identical work, the slip casting technique also requires the use of plaster moulds. The moulds are one piece for "drop out" shapes and multiple, keyed piece moulds for any other shapes. The moulds are held together with rubber bands or slices of car inner tube (see Slim Raku Vessels project).

■ An extra piece or collar of plaster, called a "spare", is designed to fit onto the mould at the point where the slip is poured into the mould. This spare acts as a reservoir of extra casting slip above the level of the top of the cast piece. The spare has two purposes. It cuts down the necessity for continual topping up of the slip as it is taken up by the porous mould walls and, because the spare retains this reservoir of slip, a constant pressure is created as the slip level sinks as it dries ensuring an even wall of clay throughout the entire area of the cast piece. A spare is only designed into moulds that are made specifically for slip casting.

Casting slip is available ready made from ceramic suppliers, or you can make up your own from suitable plastic clay or dry clay materials with a slip blunger (see Equipment, mouldmaking). Casting slip differs from a decorating slip as it contains a deflocculating agent, such as sodium silicate or carbonate. These enable a great quantity of clay to be held in a small amount of water by altering its composition while still allowing the clay to flow freely. The particles then remain in suspension when the slip is poured.

Making up casting slip is part science, part trial and error. It has three main qualities – density, fluidity and thixotropy. Casting slip that has been left for any length of time seems to thicken while undisturbed, however when stirred it regains its fluidity rapidly. This quality is due to thixotropy, enabling the newly formed cast to keep its shape without distortion while wet in the mould. Slip can be used to make test casts, allowing the development of casts that are lump free, do not overly wet the mould and release themselves from the mould without distortion once firmed. If adjustments are necessary, the litre/pint weight of the casting slip should be measured to get a density reading while accurate measurement of fluidity and thixotropy require a torsion viscometer.

After some use, the moulds begin to wear away because of the alkaline quality of the casting slip. This is most notable on precise or angular forms. Frequently used moulds will therefore need to be replaced.

INSECTAPLANT AND FLOWER (55 CM/21½ IN) COMBINED SLIPCASTING AND HAND BUILDING. MOULDS ARE MADE FROM FOUND OBJECTS, SUCH AS STONES AND VEGETABLES, WHICH ARE THEN CAST AND ASSEMBLED AT LEATHERHARD STAGE. HANDMADE ELEMENTS ARE ADDED (JENNY ORCHARD).

**Casting a slip piece**

**1** Sieve the prepared casting slip into a bucket. Quickly pour it into the dry mould in one operation. The mould is often spun on a whirler (banding wheel) while it is filled to help disperse the casting slip quickly and to prevent horizontal lines forming on the piece. This also prevents trapped air bubbles, causing another casting fault called pinholing.

CYLINDER (12 CM/4½ IN) SLIPCAST WITH PORCELAIN AND DECORATED WITH YELLOW, JAPANESE RED AND BLACK. THESE PIECES ARE OFTEN FIRED SEVERAL TIMES, RESULTING IN THE CLAY BECOMING MORE TRANSPARENT, AS WELL AS MORE VULNERABLE (BODIL MANZ).

**2** When the wall of the cast piece is sufficiently thick, pour the excess slip away for reuse and leave the mould inverted over a rack or support to let final drips drain away into a collecting tray. Leave the piece in the mould until it is leatherhard. At this point trim away with a knife the excess collar of clay formed in the spare.

**3** Remove the piece from the mould and leave it to dry. Clean it up by fettling away the seam scars with a knife and wiping it with a damp sponge. Wear a mask for large volumes of fettling and hold the work under dust extraction equipment to protect yourself from dust inhalation. Work can be fettled at the leatherhard stage, but you will achieve a less satisfactory finish.

# GLAZING AND FIRING

**GLAZING AND FIRING** ARE IN THEMSELVES DISTINCT AREAS WHEREIN THE SKILLED POTTER HAS A GREAT DEAL OF SCOPE FOR CREATIVITY AND ORIGINALITY. THEY ARE ALSO, HOWEVER, SKILLS OF WHICH A BASIC UNDERSTANDING IS VITAL IN ORDER FOR THE HANDBUILDER'S VISION TO TAKE SHAPE. WITH EACH NEW FIRING TECHNIQUE AND EACH NEW GLAZE RECIPE, KEEP A RECORD OF WHAT YOU DO AND OF THE FIRED RESULT TO HELP TO BUILD UP A REFERENCE OF SURFACE EFFECTS TO DRAW ON WHEN PLANNING NEW WORK.

# TECHNIQUES

**GLAZING** The sensitive application of glaze will enhance the colour, texture and design of a piece of work. However, the main practical reason for coating the entire surface of a domestic clay piece with glaze is to ensure that it is watertight, so that it can be cleaned easily and is safe to use for storing or presenting food or drink. The glazing technique you choose will depend on what you are glazing and how much glaze is available. The most suitable technique and the thickness of application is also dictated by the nature of the glaze you are using.

## Glazing the inside of an enclosed shape

Enclosed internal surfaces should be glazed before any external glazing or colour decoration is undertaken. This prevents any unnecessary handling of applied external, unfired powdery materials or marring of carefully applied, unfired designs and glaze.

**1** First stir the glaze thoroughly and check its consistency. Fill a jug (pitcher) and pour the glaze into the piece of work. Pour in enough glaze to fill the vessel as quickly as possible.

**2** While turning the work in both hands, immediately pour out the excess back into the bucket making sure you have covered the entire surface of the inside wall. Any small spots you miss can be touched up using a soft brush or glaze mop and any excess spilled over onto the outside wall can be wiped back with a damp sponge.

The reason for performing this task with speed is to prevent the wall from becoming saturated. If this happens the glaze applied to the outer wall will not adhere. The wall will act like a wet sponge that cannot take up any more water, and the capillary action caused by the porosity of the bisqued wall will cease, therefore preventing the glaze particles forming an even covering to the surface of the work. If a piece does become over saturated either leave it until dry and then continue with the glazing or speed dry the work with a heat source, such as a paint stripper gun.

JUG (23 CM/9 IN)
PORCELAIN THROWN AND
MODELLED, WITH SLIP AND GLAZE
(EMMANUEL COOPER).

## Glazing the outside of an enclosed shape

The work should be held in as few places as possible – at the foot or base to prevent unnecessary fingermarks of omitted glaze. Alternatively, and where possible, use a glazing claw (see Equipment, glaze and decoration) particularly if a piece is awkward to hold or the glaze is susceptible to marking because it does not "flatten out" in the firing.

**1** Hold the work upside down and level to the surface of the glaze as it is submerged so a pocket of air is trapped inside, preventing a double build-up of glaze to the inside wall. Immerse it in the glaze quickly for no longer than three seconds to the point to which you want the glaze to reach.

You could also dip the piece base down, holding onto the dry inside wall. This enables you to use a different or contrasting glaze on the external wall, which will finish to a clean line at the rim edge. Plunge the piece in to the required depth of glaze for a maximum of 3 seconds being careful not to let glaze cascade over the top edge.

When removing the piece, tilt it to let any excess glaze drip back into the bucket giving it a slight shake to help any last drips fall away.

**2** Slide the wet glazed piece onto the edge of a board or table rim being careful not to touch the wet glaze, and allow it to dry before it is handled again. If there are any missing spots, fill them in using a soft brush.

**3** When the glaze is bone dry, you can pare away any touched-up finger marks or glaze drips with the edge of a metal kidney or rub them down with a dry finger tip bringing the powdered glaze to an even level. Pinholes in the powdery glaze surface can also be rubbed down with a dry finger once the glaze is thoroughly dry, but this is often unnecessary for fluid glazes will smooth out in the firing.

**4** If required, a second overlapping layer of glaze (or selectively dipped areas) can be applied in the same way. This double dipping technique will affect the fired result and such overlapping glazes should be test fired first to ensure that one glaze does not cause the other to overly flux and run in the firing.

THROWN SKIRTED BOWL
(25.5 CM/10¼IN)
A CLAY MIXTURE OF RED
EARTHENWARE AND STONEWARE
WITH VERY COARSE GROG. GLAZES
ARE DIPPED AND SPRAYED AND THE
PIECE IS THEN OXIDATION FIRED
(RAY SILVERMAN).
PHOTOGRAPH BY HOWARD SHOOTER.

## Dipping a tile or small object

Small objects are dipped using the same technique as glazing the outside of an enclosed shape. If glazing a number of small objects ensure the glaze is stirred frequently as glaze allowed to settle, even for a short time, will not give an adequate covering.

Eggcups, for example, can be dipped with a quick once up and down jerking action while under the glaze to dispel the trapped air pocket and pull glaze over the internal walls.

## Pouring glaze for external walls

It is often easier to use a pouring technique for glazing ceramic pieces. This might be suitable if there is insufficient glaze to fully immerse a large piece of work, if spraying equipment is not available or if the glaze is inappropriate for brushing.

Invert the piece, resting it on level slats over a large container. Pour glaze down the side of the piece, covering as much of the surface as possible. Try not to overlap the glaze unless this is effect you desire. Small, missed areas can be spot patched rather than making the applied glaze overly thick.

Glazing external walls in this way tends to cause drops of dried glaze to accumulate at the rim and around any points that are resting on the slats, so it can be a laborious technique that requires careful scraping once the glaze is dry to level the surface. To avoid unnecessary handling, wipe the bases clean of glaze while the piece is still inverted. The powdered glaze will damage when dry, particularly at the top edge or rim if it is knocked.

Overlapping the glaze by pouring it onto a piece of work gives a multi-coloured effect where the thicknesses vary.

## Glazing open shapes

**1** Glaze the top face of a plate, saucer or any other flat shape first. If you do not have a glaze claw and there is not enough glaze to fully immerse the open shape, the glaze should first be poured on the front face, tilting the edges and using a swilling motion to cover the surface. The excess is poured out and splashes to the back face wiped back after the piece has been allowed to become dry to the touch.

**2** To glaze the bottom face of an open shape, immerse it by holding the rim in two places and supporting the back with your thumbs.

If there is a foot rim you can hold, this is the better alternative, leaving fewer fingermarks to be retouched. Alternatively the back face can be poured one section at a time allowing the first to become dry to the touch before moving onto the next.

**3** Alternatively, glaze claws are particularly useful for glazing flatware, such as plates and saucers, which cannot be easily held. Hold the piece with a glazing claw and sweep it with one motion through the glaze.

## Spraying Glaze

Spraying is normally used to apply a "difficult" glaze that will not fire flat or that needs to be applied extremely thinly in a controlled manner. It is also often used when a soft, blurred, "disappearing" effect is required to edges of areas of coloured glaze. This is also a useful method of applying glaze when the work is too heavy or awkward to lift, or when there is insufficient glaze for individual, large pieces of work.

As with all glaze application, spraying should be done only when wearing an appropriate mask (respirator) and using extraction equipment (see Equipment, glaze and decoration and health and safety) as particles of airborne glaze materials should never be inhaled. Build up the glaze evenly, turning the piece of work on a banding wheel and holding the gun at an adequate distance to allow a wide spray that does not spot patch. After use, ensure that you wash spraying equipment with water to prevent the nozzle clogging up with glaze.

A transparent glaze is sprayed onto the textured interior of a work. This enables a thin, even application, which suits the nature of a transparent glaze. Pouring glaze on this piece would have resulted in pools of glaze collecting in the low points of the texture. Other "difficult" types of glaze that should be applied by spraying include those with a matt-fired finish.

| Brushing a glaze | Wax resist | Cleaning back glaze |
|---|---|---|

There are many brush-on glazes sold commercially in many colours, surfaces, fired effects and temperature ranges. They have a similar consistency to non-drip emulsion (latex) paint and are therefore easier to apply with a stiff brush. For a covering equivalent to poured or dipped glaze you will need to apply at least two coats, allowing the first to dry first.

These glazes are useful when using a small amount of glaze or if you require a particular colour or effect. Many slop glazes can be applied with a soft brush as an overall covering or as decoration. Glazes made up from dry materials should be tested for brushing as the technique can appear patchy and uneven.

Wax resist solution or hot candle wax melted with equal parts of paraffin oil (or kerosene) can be banded onto footrings (feet), bases and lid galleries to give a clean edge to the applied glaze and to make the important task of wiping back less laborious. Ensure the wax resist solution is completely dry before applying the glaze so it will repel the glaze. Candle wax and oil is an inflammable mixture and can easily catch fire if it gets too hot. If this happens smother flames with a fireproof material and remove the heat source immediately. Do not pour on water or use a fire extinguisher.

Any glaze must be cleared away from lid fittings where lids are to be fired in place to ensure a good fit. Bases, edges or points that will touch a kiln shelf should also be wiped clean with a damp sponge. This process is crucial to avoid the fired piece becoming stuck to a kiln shelf.

Spout strainer holes and lid air holes for teapots should be cleared of glaze before firing to prevent the fired gaze permanently filling holes that should be open. Do this, once the glaze is dry, with a needle or hole cutter.

Glaze can be left on a base if the piece to be fired is set on a stilt. Razor-sharp stilt scars can be removed using a carborundum stone (kiln brick bits) after firing.

# TECHNIQUES
# KILN FIRING
Once any forming and decorating work is complete the piece must next undergo the firing process to bring about ceramic change. The red heat and beyond within a kiln alters the nature of clay and glaze materials both chemically and physically causing them to become hard and permanent. Unless you are firing using an electric kiln with a control system, firing involves vigilance and attendance, often over a long period of time.

■ Many potters fire their work to an initial biscuit (bisque) firing of around 980–1100°C (1796–2012°F) to make the ware porous and give physical strength before decoration and glazing. The higher the temperature, the less porous the clay becomes. Some potters, who glaze fire to a low glaze temperature, such as raku or low earthenware, use an industrial technique of hard biscuit or bisque firing, when the initial firing has a higher temperature than that following glaze firing. This method provides a more vitrified clay body on low-fired glazed work, but can introduce the hurdle of applying glaze to work that is no longer porous. To overcome this, the high-fired bisque work can be heated in the kiln to enable a slop glaze to adhere to its surface.

Other potters omit the biscuit (bisque) firing process altogether and prefer to single fire. This shortens the long wait for the finished result and cuts out additional firing cost and handling time.

Temperature rise will vary widely depending on the type and size of your kiln, as well as the size of the work and the density of the kiln pack, so use the firing chart at the end of this section as a rough guide to firing times only.

SALTGLAZED JAR WITH A
CURL (35 CM/14 IN)
SINGLE FIRED, WITH COBALT AND
TITANIUM SLIPS (JANE HAMLYN).

## Biscuit firing (or single firing)

Before any work can be fired it must first be allowed to become completely bone dry. Larger or thicker pieces of work must be left for longer to dry. The drying process is completed in the initial stages of the biscuit (bisque) firing known as "water smoking" – when, at 100–600°C (212–1112°F), chemically combined water evaporates and is driven out as steam. During this stage, vents in the kiln are left open to allow steam to exit.

It is critical to proceed slowly at this drying phase – too much haste will cause the steam to push open or explode the work. This creates a low, thudding sound in the kiln and is the death knell of probably all pieces of work in the kiln. Large or small pieces with thick wall sections – over 5 mm (¼ in) – are particularly susceptible to this, so take care. Leaving a biscuit (bisque) firing on a low temperature overnight with the kiln vents open is a good way to ensure work is safe to be heated further.

Once the initial firing has reached beyond 600°C (1112°F) or red heat, it is safe to turn up the heating rate, close any vents and proceed to the final temperature (see firing times and temperatures). The kiln is then allowed to cool and can be opened for unpacking when the temperature has reached around 100–150°C (212–302°F).

## Heating and cooling for glaze

As the kiln reaches certain temperatures (227°C/440°F and 557°C/1034°F) chemical changes take place that increase the size and formation of the quartz crystals in the clay. The first at 225°C (437°F) is known as the "cristobolite inversion" or "squeeze", the second at 573°C (1063°F) is known as the "quartz inversion". This quartz crystal change then repeats in reverse at the cooling stage. Particular care must be taken not to hurry the cooling of a glaze firing kiln at and around these temperatures by prematurely opening vents and doors. Doing so will result in fine cracks or dunting appearing. Sharp-edged cracks appear during the cooling process, whereas rounded or smooth edged cracks occur during the heating process.

## Glaze firing

The final temperature for a glaze firing is predetermined by the glaze and clay body of the fired work. Glaze firing should be started slowly to drive out any moisture taken into the biscuit (bisque) ware from glazing. When the kiln is glowing at red heat or 600°C (1112°F), the rate of climb can be increased and vents should be closed.

When a glaze is subjected to heat, it interacts and fuses not only within itself, but also with materials on the clay surface it lies on. This is particularly the case in high-fired temperature or stoneware glazes. This reaction with the clay surface, called "interface", secures the glaze onto the clay. At low-fired, or earthenware, temperatures there is less interface of the glaze and clay.

The effect of heat on a glaze is subject to the amount of time a firing takes to achieve final temperature. This combination of time and heat is known as "heatwork" and it can only accurately be measured by pyrometric temperature cones or bars. Heat can also be gauged visually by colour, but shield your eyes with protective goggles and avoid staring into the glow of a high temperature kiln for long

periods. At 1100°C (2012°F) the colour is orangey red, at 1200°C (2192°F) the orange brightens and at 1260°C (2300°F) it becomes bright yellow.

As the temperature rises, vitrification occurs when the clay and glaze or colours compact and fuse. As the final glaze temperature nears, glaze bubbles and craters form as gas escapes, which can cause the glaze defects of bloating or pinholing if it is not allowed to settle. By sustaining the kiln heat at a constant temperature, known as soaking, these defects can be eliminated. The kiln can then be turned off to cool.

## Crystalline glaze firing

The rate at which the temperature is decreased determines the final size of crystals in a glaze. Crystalline glazes require a top maturing temperature of 1260–1280°C (2300–2336°F) followed by a rapid cool to 1100°C (2012°F) and then a prolonged soak to 1040°C (1904°F) to create seeds for the growth of crystals. Pieces of crystal glazed work are packed onto a foot or saucer to catch running glaze and glaze drips, which are ground off with a grindstone after firing.

## Glaze temperature ranges

The temperature of a glaze firing varies according to the clay used in the piece. The ranges for earthenware, stoneware, porcelain and bone china are as follows:

- Earthenware 950–1150°C (1742–2102°F)
- Stoneware and porcelain 1200–1300°C (2192–2372°F)
- Bone china 1080–1100°C (1976–2012°F)

SLICED LOTUS FRUIT OF YOUR DREAMS, DETAIL OF CRYSTALLINE GLAZE (KATE MALONE).

SLICED LOTUS FRUIT OF YOUR DREAMS (38 CM/15 IN). COIL BUILT IN T-MATERIAL CLAY, CRYSTALLINE GLAZE FIRED (KATE MALONE). PHOTOGRAPH BY STEPHEN BRAYNE.

## Reduction firing

All kilns are capable of providing an oxidizing atmosphere around the ware during firing – this is where the circulation of air passing through the kiln is unrestricted. However, not all kilns are able to produce a second type of atmosphere, called "reduction", which involves restricting the passage of secondary air into the kiln and controlling pressure in the firing chamber with a flue damper. Reduction firing, used in conjunction with high temperature glazes or to produce lustreware, is achieved in kilns that supply heat through a burnt fuel, such as wood, oil, gas and solid fuels.

The picture shows a reduction flame at the spyhole of a gas-fired kiln. The strength of reduction is judged by the length and colour of the flame that protrudes when a bung is temporarily removed from a spyhole in the door, and the amount of smoke coming from the chimney.

During reduction, the kiln's atmosphere seeks out oxygen to enable it to burn. Because the oxygen supply is restricted, the atmosphere grabs the chemically combined oxygen in some of the metal oxides contained in clay and glaze, producing an array of reduction effects, such as copper turning blood red, precious metals becoming lustrous and iron spot crystals being drawn from clay into the glaze surface.

## Enamel firing

Onglazes fuse with the glaze on which they are applied at low temperatures. The temperatures can vary according to the colours used. This firing involves fusing colour into the softened glaze, often using successive firings to create overlapping mixed hues and depth of colour. Firings are relatively fast and require the opening of the kiln vent to allow fumes caused by the burning of painted mediums to leave the kiln as they burn away.

Enamel firing temperatures range from 700–900°C (1292–1652°F).

CONICAL TEAPOT CUP (13 CM/5 IN) CAST AND HANDBUILT IN SEMI-PORCELAIN CLAY. BISCUIT (BISQUE) FIRED, GLAZED IN A SEMI-MATT GLAZE AND PAINTED WITH ONGLAZE ENAMELS WITH SGRAFFITO DRAWING (MARGARET FORDE).

## Raku firing

A traditional Japanese firing technique, raku is when glazed, biscuit-fired decorative ware is taken to its firing temperature very quickly. This produces a characteristic crazed quality to a glaze and lustrous effects to copper glazes. The hot work can be left uncovered to oxidize, quenched in water or quickly smothered in a combustible material, such as sawdust, to reduce the work. The clays used to produce work for raku firing are always open so they can withstand the thermal shock of the firing and cooling process (see Clay: The Fundamental Ingredient). Raku is exciting with its spontaneous immediacy and its delicate blend of control and experiment.

Kilns can vary from an electric kiln to a brick-lined kiln such as the one used in the Slim Raku Vessels project. A downdraft kiln such as this one draws air down a separate stack on the side of the kiln, giving a more even temperature throughout the kiln and allowing the layering of work with shelves. An updraft kiln with shelves may tend to trap the heat, causing uneven temperatures throughout the kiln, although this can be overcome if there is a gap around the outer edge of the kiln shelf.

Raku firing temperatures range from 900–1000°C (1652–1832°F).

Raku kilns should be fired outdoors because a good deal of smoke will invariably be generated when unloading the fired items into the sawdust for reduction.

## Vapour firing

Salt, soda and wood firing are all types of vapour glazing. In order for salt glaze to develop, the clay body or applied slips must contain a certain proportion of silica, which is softened by the heat of the kiln and fuses with the sodium or salt. Salt firing is a toxic process producing hydrochloric acid fumes as a by-product so many makers who vapour glaze opt for the less polluting option of soda firing, which is less corrosive to the kiln and produces softer and brighter colours.

Salt and soda glazing produce effects ranging from the characteristic orange-peel texture covering the entire external area or partial flashing. The results depend on the design of the kiln, the kiln pack and the amount of vapour created. Pots and lid fittings are packed into the kiln on small wads made from a mixture of three parts alumina hydrate to one part china clay held together with a proportion of flour to make it into a kneadable dough.

The glaze melt is used as a visual indication of when to remove the work from the kiln while it is still red hot.

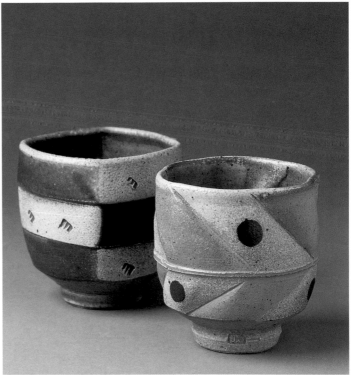

Tea Bowls (10 cm/4 in) thrown and soda fired (Jeff Oestreich).

The allure of wood firing has as much to do with the physical process as the characteristic flashing and finished texture of the fire-glazed clay. The minerals in the ash deposits interact with the minerals in the clay, which fuse and form the glaze to the exposed surfaces of clay in the kiln firing. Wood is not only used as a kiln fuel for vapour glazing, it is often chosen as a fuel because it is readily available. The wood-firing process requires a constant vigil to maintain a steady temperature rise and to create the desired kiln atmosphere. For larger kilns this requires teams of wood stokers to maintain kilns, such as the "snake" or "climbing" kilns used in Japan.

Salt or soda is drip fed, sprayed or thrown into the flame of a kiln or through spyholes around the firing chamber at around 1240°C (2264°F).

Test rings, made of the same clay and coated with the same slips as the work you are firing are placed in the kiln in an accessible place. They are extracted to assess how much glaze has formed on the work and whether more vapour is required. Test rings are often placed in more than one area of a kiln because of temperature variations.

## Sawdust and smoking

Pits or metal bins are packed with a combustible material, usually sawdust, around work for this low firing technique, which produces a characteristic patchy, black carbon effect. It is a technique often combined with burnished pieces and, although it seems to be low tech, it requires fine judgement on how best to pack the work and when to remove it. Work is often biscuit (bisque) fired before being placed for firing, which, if carefully controlled, can be successfully carried out on any clay body.

Glazed work can also be smoke fumed by exposing the fired piece to a reduction atmosphere inside a saggar packed with combustible material. A saggar is a lidded refractory box that protects fired work from direct contact with the kiln's atmosphere. This enables work to be reduced within an electric or oxidized environment with a greater control of the heating and cooling process. Ensure that the kiln and the immediate environment are well ventilated for this process.

WORK BY DUNCAN AYSCOUGH REDUCING AFTER A SAWDUST FIRING.

VASE (18 CM/7 IN) COILED, BURNISHED AND SMOKE FIRED (JANE PERRYMAN).

## Firing times and temperatures

This chart gives examples of firing times for biscuit (bisque) and single firing, glaze firing, raku firing, crystalline firing and enamel firing. They relate to the number of hours the firings take to achieve certain temperatures and the specific temperature points at which the kiln atmosphere requires soaking or reducing. The term "soak" means holding a temperature in position.

| | Reduction for glaze firing temperatures can commence from 1000°C (1832°F) and continue until 1350°C (2462°F) for porcelain. *Italics* refer to cooling temperatures. | | | | |
|---|---|---|---|---|---|
| HOURS | BISCUIT (BISQUE) AND SINGLE | GLAZE (REDUCTION & OXIDIZED) | RAKU | CRYSTALLINE | ENAMEL |
| 1 | 50°C (122°F) | 50°C (122°F) | 300°C (572°F) | 50°C (122°F) | 50°C (122°F) |
| 2 | 100°C (212°F) | 100°C (212°F) | 1000°C (1832°F) /reduction | 100°C (212°F) | 100°C (212°F) |
| 3 | 150°C (302°F) | 150°C (302°F) | 100°C (212°F) | 150°C (302°F) | 150°C (302°F) |
| 4 | 200°C (392°F) | 250°C (482°F) | | 250°C (482°F) | 250°C (482°F) |
| 5 | 300°C (572°F) | 400°C (752°F) | | 400°C (752°F) | 400°C (752°F) |
| 6 | 400°C (752°F) | 700°C (1292°F) | | 700°C (1292°F) | 700°C (1292°F) |
| 7 | 600°C (1112°F) | 1000°C+ (1832°F+) Reduction, soak at top earthware temp | | 1260–80°C (2300–36°F) (top temperature variable) | 600°C (1112°F) |
| 8 | 700°C (1292°F) | 1280°C (2336°F) Reduction, soak at top stoneware temp | | Rapid cool from top temperature to 1100°C (2012°F) | 400°C (752°F) |
| 9 | 880°C (1616°F) | 1350°C (2462°F) Reduction soak porcelain | | 1040°C (1904°F) soak | 300°C (572°F) |
| 10 | 1000°C (1832°F) Top temp biscuit | 1250°C (2280°F) | | 1040°C (1904°F) | 200°C (392°F) soak |
| 11 | 800°C (1472°F) | 1000°C (1832°F) | | 1040°C (1904°F) soak | 100°C (212°F) |
| 12 | 600°C (1112°F) | 700°C (1292°F) | | 1040°C (1904°F) soak | |
| 13 | 400°C (752°F) | 400°C (752°F) | | Begin to cool | |
| 14 | 300°C (572°F) | 200°C (392°F) | | 900°C (1652°F) | |
| 15 | 200°C (392°F) | 100°C (212°F) | | 500°C (932°F) | |
| 16 | 100°C (212°F) | | | 300°C (572°F) | |
| 17 | | | | 150°C (302°F) | |

# PROJECTS

**THE FOLLOWING CHAPTER COMPRISES 13 PROJECTS** FOR YOU TO UNDERTAKE IN THE STUDIO. EACH ONE IS THE UNIQUE VISION OF THE ARTIST, AND THEREFORE REPRESENTS AN IDEAL OPPORTUNITY TO TRACE THE CREATIVE PROCESS FROM THE EARLIEST STAGES OF INSPIRATION AND DESIGN THROUGH TO THE FINAL EXECUTION. THE TECHNIQUES USED IN THE PROJECTS ARE SPECIFICALLY INTENDED TO COINCIDE WITH THOSE DESCRIBED IN THE PREVIOUS CHAPTERS.

# Raku Bug

In this project Jola Spytkowska has assembled a selection of nails, screws, a hinge and other items from her junk box to make a creature that resembles an insect. Through drawing she has explored and modified the shapes. Once the idea had developed it became clear that pinching and coiling were the ideal techniques to form the piece.

**Materials**
White St Thomas clay

**Equipment**
Box of junk
Sketchbook
Pencil and colour pens
Potter's knife
Toothbrush
Sponge
Rolling pin
Wooden tool
Narrow pointed tool
Paintbrushes
Electric kiln
Raku kiln
Gas bottle (propane tank)
Thick leather gloves
Protective goggles
Purpose-made tongs
Metal bucket
Sawdust
Wire wool (for cleaning off
    burnt sawdust)

**Glaze**
Commercially prepared
    brush-on glazes

**Firing**
Biscuit (bisque) fire to 1080°C
    (1976°F)
    60°C (140°F)
    300°C (572°F)
    120°C (248°F)
    1080°C (1976°F)
Glaze fire to 990–1040°C
    (1814–1904°F)

**1** Design your creature. Outline your drawing in black ink and then colour it. The drawing will enable you to decide what you need to make and how to make it. Do this by looking at its separate parts.

**2** Make the body by pinching out two lemon-shaped, shallow forms of equal size. When these have become leatherhard, score up the edges, add slurry (see using slurry for joining) and join firmly. Make small air holes.

**3** Prepare the flange that will go around the edge of the body. Roll out a long coil about 5 mm (¼in) thick and very lightly flatten this coil with a rolling pin.

**4** Cut the flattened coil in two. Join the flanges to the edge of the body with slurry, pressing firmly. Cut the edges where the two flanges meet so that they join without a gap.

**5** Prepare the legs. Roll out a long coil and cut into six sections. Curve them. Roll out six small balls of clay for the feet, flatten them a little and then join them onto the legs with slurry. Leave the legs to become leatherhard.

**6** Roll out another coil for the spine. Join it onto the body. Take the edge of a wooden tool and impress it into the spine at regular intervals to imitate the form of a hinge.

**7** Roll out a short coil for the tail, which is narrow and pointed at one end. Curl round the pointed end. When it is leatherhard join the tail to the main body.

**8** Roll out a small coil for the antennae and curve it into a U-shape. Add small balls of clay to the ends and pierce holes through them.

**9** Join the legs to the body when they have become leatherhard. Score and slurry first then press them down firmly and smooth around the joins. Stand the bug upright and adjust the legs so that they touch the surface of the table. Add eight little balls of clay around the flange. Impress them with a narrow pointed tool to imitate screws.

**10** Finish off the bug by adding the eyes. Make two small balls of clay, flatten them slightly, attach to the body and impress them with the head of a screw. Biscuit (bisque) fire to 1080°C (1976°F).

**11** Outline the bug all over with a pencil around the edges. These edges will remain unglazed. The unglazed areas will smoke a charcoal black in the sawdust, to recreate something of the effect of the black ink in your original drawings.

**12** Choose the appropriate colour glazes. Those used in this project fire to a low temperature which makes them suitable for raku. Apply three coats of each colour. When ready, fire the bug in the raku kiln. Remember to wear protective gloves and goggles. When the temperature reaches 1000°C (1832°F) remove the kiln lid and lift out the bug with purpose-made tongs. Place it in a metal bucket full of sawdust and leave it to smoke for about 15 minutes. Remove and cool it before cleaning and scrubbing gently with wire wool.

# Balancing Tricks

These figures by Josie Warshaw use pinching, coiling and modelling techniques. Photographs of modelled "balancing tricks" by her young son were used as a reference to develop the forms in clay. You could decide to give a figurative piece a different emphasis by also modelling a head and further body details. The approach used here is particularly effective for capturing the feeling of movement.

## Materials
50% T-material clay (or any
    grogged white clay)
50% White earthenware
    (mixed together).

## Equipment
Paddle
Toothbrush
Sponge
Potter's knife
Wooden modelling tool
Paint stripper gun
Hacksaw blade
Metal kidney
Plastic sheet
Gloves for glazing
Raku kiln
Gas bottle (propane tank)
Thick leather gloves
Protective goggles
Purpose-made tongs
Metal bucket
Sawdust
Wire wool

## Glaze
WHITE GLAZE
| | |
|---|---|
| High alkaline frit | 95% |
| SMD ball clay | 5% |
| COLOUR ADDITIONS | |
| Tin oxide | 6% |
| Bentonite | 1% |

## Firing
Biscuit (bisque) fire to 1000°C
    (1832°F)
Raku fire to approximately
    1000°C (1832°F) or until
    the glaze looks fluxed

**1** Form the lower half of the figure up to waist level by making a pinched cup, using plastic clay. Make tucks in the clay and squeeze them together to narrow the neck of the pinched cup, keeping the edge thick in preparation to take the applied coils at the next stage.

**2** Use a paddle to alter the shape until there is an approximate feel of the contours of the body, which will be refined at the paring stage. Next, tap the base on the flat working surface to tip the cup backwards, giving it a leaning movement. Ease the shape from the inside using your fingertips to belly the shape out. Leave it to become leatherhard.

**3** Remove pieces of V-shaped cuts along the edge to bring in the shape of the body and rejoin with the slurry and score method (see using slurry for joining). Pinch up the top edge to lengthen the shape and to achieve the contour and direction of the body.

**4** Add coils to extend the body and bring the shape in or out where necessary. Because the top working edge is leatherhard, slurry and score it to attach the first coil. Pinch and smear all the subsequent coils into place – use a modelling tool on the internal side of the wall, but use a finger tip to smear down the coils on the external wall.

**5** Join two circles of coils to form the legs, slurrying and scoring them into place. To complete this in one sitting, speed-firm the first coils with a paint stripper gun so that the weight and direction of the subsequent coils are supported.

**6** Apply further coils to extend the legs. Check their shape, angle and proportions as you go along.

**7** Use a small modelling tool with a rounded end to join the internal wall of the leg coils.

**8** Pare the surface of the figure with a hacksaw blade to accentuate the contours and to even the external wall.

**9** Remove the hacksaw blade marks with a metal kidney and further accentuate the contours of the figure.

**10** Build up the feet with small coils and push them together with the small wooden tool. Close in the soles of the feet with a flat piece of clay joined on the external wall. Model the feet with a hacksaw blade and metal kidney. Cover the whole figure in plastic and leave it until it becomes leatherhard. Finally even out the surface and contours with a hacksaw blade and metal kidney, and wipe with a damp sponge. When the work is bone dry biscuit (bisque) fire it to 1000°C (1832°F).

**11** Pour a fairly thick layer of white raku glaze over the biscuit (bisque) fired figure and wipe the resting points clean of any glaze with a damp sponge. Raku fire the figure to around 1000°C (1832°F), or until the glaze looks melted. Remove it from the kiln with tongs while it is still red and reduce it in sawdust where it will smoulder until it is cool. Remove the loose carbon left on the surface from the sawdust reduction with wire wool.

# Full-Bellied Coiled Pot

This pot by Sarah Scampton uses a simple coiling technique, ideal for creating shapes that form themselves with a minimum of interference. With its seamless, continuous rhythm, coiling allows the form to simply emerge and you need to use no tools except for your hands.

## Materials
Clay C-material or T-material
Earthenware (can make up to
⅓ of mix)

## Equipment
Round kiln shelf or bat
Banding wheel
Sponge
Paint stripper gun
Potter's knife
Small brush
Clay props
Wooden modelling tool
Paddle
Gloves for glazing
Brushes for glazes
Electric kiln

## Glaze
BASIC SLIP – GORDON BALDWINS
500 g (18 oz) Black ball clay
500 g (18 oz) China clay
200 g (7 oz) Borax frit
Oxides and underglaze
colours
Multiple layers are painted on
by brush until the required
depth is achieved.

## Firing
Biscuit (bisque) fire to 1000°C
(1832°F)
Glaze fire to between
1120–1180°C
(2048–2156°F)

**1** Place your round kiln shelf or bat on the banding wheel. Wet the area around the outside edge of a round kiln shelf or bat. Apply a thin coil, squeezing it onto the shelf so that it sticks.

**2** Make sure the clay is soft enough to add to the next layer without too much pressure and no water. Continue to add coils on the inside of the edge so that the diameter gets smaller and smaller until you have six or more layers.

**3** Use the edge of your index finger to stroke the inside to keep the shape full while you support the outside with the whole of your other hand. Take a paint stripper gun and gently dry the clay until it is just firm.

**4** Brush the edge of the coil with water then add the next coil. Make sure that the coils are really well joined together as this could become a weak spot in the finished pot.

**5** Think about the emerging shape as you add the coils and decide whether you want to change the inwards angle.

**6** At this point a dome shape appears and the inwards angle becomes much steeper. You should now dry off the clay more often, particularly if it becomes too floppy.

**9** Turning the pot is a tricky manoeuvre. First slip a knife between the kiln shelf and the first coil, working your way around until the clay is no longer stuck to the shelf. Gently slide the pot towards you, maintaining its shape until one third is beyond the edge of the kiln shelf. Do not let go of the pot! Put one arm inside the pot and spread your fingertips around the inside of the rim. Gently lift the pot off the shelf and turn it over in your arms.

**7** Close off the form to the desired diameter then add more coils to form a rim. Add these almost vertically. Coil the rim higher than you need.

**8** Trim the rim to just below the chosen level, straightening it with a sharp knife, then add the final coil that should fit neatly around in one length. Dry the pot until leatherhard, when it will be ready to turn over.

**10** Carefully lower it back onto the kiln shelf on its rim. You may have to use clay props under the rim.

**11** Cut off the first coil of this new uppermost edge. It is usually thicker so when removed, it is easier to join on to the subsequent coils. You are now working inwards towards the base of the pot.

**12** Wet the edge and start coiling. Make sure that the first join between the leatherhard clay and the soft clay is good. Squeeze the clay around the same joint several times.

**13** Continue to work in towards the base, checking the profile of your pot. You can trim off any section at any time and rebuild, but this can put a kink in the natural flow of the developing shape.

**14** As your aperture becomes smaller, it may be necessary to go over the areas again. Continuous pressing between fingers and thumb, pincer-like, creates the texture and strength.

**15** You should have a small hole left in the base. Dry round this area until it is firm, then brush the edge with water.

**16** Make a small pad of clay roughly the size of the hole. Trim it to the shape of the hole and place it over the gap and work in the edges with a wooden tool. You may have to beat the base with a paddle to get it flat.

**17** Dry the base to leatherhard then turn the pot over again, keeping it well supported.

**18** Push some clay props underneath the pot before removing both your hands. Put one hand into the pot and push the inside of the base area against the kiln shelf to make sure it balances. It is often worth biscuit (bisque) firing the pot with the props in place to prevent it slumping. Apply the glazes wearing gloves and glaze fire the pot.

# Coiled Snake

This coiled, inlaid and burnished snake was made by Josie Warshaw in memory of a friend's departure to Australia. The construction technique combines pinching and coiling, starting from a pinched cup and building up the form with coils using the score and slurry method. The snake's shape forms an interesting surface on which to apply a repeat decoration with inlaying and burnishing, giving a finished effect that is reminiscent of an actual snakeskin.

## Materials
Grogged Red Earthenware

## Equipment
Paddle
Potter's knife
Hooped (trimming) tool
Hacksaw blade
Wooden modelling tools
Needle
Toothbrush
Kiln shelf
Small mouse-shaped flexible
    metal kidney
Wooden stick
Paintbrush
Face mask (respirator) and
    gloves
Burnishing tool
Clear wax
Soft cloth
Electric kiln

## Slip
| | |
|---|---|
| SM ball clay | 60% |
| China clay | 40% |
| COLOUR ADDITIONS | |
| Yellow stain | 10% |
| Moss green stain | 10% |
| Black stain | 10% |

## Firing
Biscuit (bisque) fire to 980°C
(1796°F)

**1** Form a pinched cup using plastic clay that is on the firm side of soft to make the head. Narrow the pinched cup considerably at the neck. Paddle the pinched shape while it is still soft to achieve the diamond-shaped head and flattened underside. Leave it to firm enough to handle without distortion, but soft enough to still move the clay. Cut a line to form the open mouth. Carve away the unevenness made by pinching on the internal area of the mouth and carve in contours using a small hooped tool. Leave the head to firm a little more before any further work.

**2** Pare the external surface and shape of the head with a hacksaw blade and then paddle it until it is the shape you require. Use small, soft, flattened coils to form the eyes, one for the eyelid and two for the eye using a wooden modelling tool. Pierce the eyes with a needle to allow excess air to escape as the piece dries. Attach and model the teeth. Use a temporary prop of clay to hold the mouth open while it firms to leatherhard.

**3** Roll plenty of coils before coiling the body so there is not a continual switch between tasks. Attach the first coil of the snake's body to the head by slurrying and scoring. Use your fingers to make the external joins and a small wooden modelling tool to make the interior joins. Make the first part of the coiled body while supporting the piece in your lap. When the body becomes too long and unwieldy, transfer it to a kiln shelf where it can stay until it has been fired. Even, smooth and reinforce all the external coil joins on the external wall with a hacksaw blade as the piece progresses.

**4** Bend the shape upwards while the body is still soft. Prop it with a clay support to create a space under which the curled body will pass. (Leave the prop in place for drying and firing then remove it.) Add coils to extend the outer curve of the acute, sideways and upward bends of the snake.

**5** Pare the body and reinforce the joins on the exterior walls using a hacksaw blade and metal kidney. Bend the body upwards while it is still soft and reinforce the joins on the underbelly of the snake – once it is leatherhard it is not possible to bend the body upwards.

**6** Make the tail end with shorter, tighter coils around a stick. Use joined sections made by the same method. Make the final point of the tail solid and knot it while still soft. Partly shape the surface with a hacksaw blade and metal kidney before joining it to the main body.

**7** Leave the snake to become leatherhard. You can then model and finish off the surface with wooden modelling tools and a small metal kidney. Carve lines into the surface to achieve the texture of snakeskin.

**8** Fill the carved lines with thick, yogurt-consistency, coloured slips in green, black and yellow using a paintbrush. Apply two or three layers. Wait for each layer to become dry to the touch before applying the next.

**9** Allow the inlaid coloured slips to firm then pare them back with the curved edge of the carving tool.

**11** Apply clear wax to the snake once it has been fired, then buff it with a soft cloth to bring it to a shine.

**10** Carefully burnish the top surface of the snake over its entire area. Leave the piece to become bone dry and biscuit (bisque) fire.

# Burnished Plate

Burnishing is the most ancient method known to decrease the porosity of fired clay. To Montse Jalon the appeal of this technique lies in the richness of the burnished surface, the simplicity of the materials required and the minimum of equipment needed to achieve its effects. Burnishing is most effective on simple, uncomplicated shapes. Be especially careful when burnishing edges, because the pressure may easily make the edge crumble.

**Materials**
Red earthenware clay

**Equipment**
Piece of canvas
Rolling pin
Two wooden slats
Plaster plate mould
Wooden spoon
Potter's knife
Steel kidney scrapers
   (serrated and stiff)
Needle or pointed tool
Brush
Smooth pebble
Polishing wax
Electric kiln

**Slip**

| | |
|---|---|
| Ball clay | 50% |
| China clay | 25% |
| Cornish stone | 10% |
| Flint | 15% |
| Cobalt Oxide | 10% |
| Black iron oxide | 12% |

**Firing**
Biscuit (bisque) fire the piece
   to 1080°C (1976°F) in an
   electric kiln

**1** There are several ways of preparing a big slab of clay. One way is to join small pieces of clay with your fingers and flatten them by hand in preparation for rolling.

**2** Using a rolling pin, roll an even slab of clay on the canvas. The slab must be big enough to cover the surface of the plate mould comfortably. Use wooden slats to determine the required thickness of the clay. Roll the clay from the centre so that it moves out easily. Keep the clay free and lift it regularly from the canvas.

**3** Lay the rolled slab of clay over the mould so that it overlaps the edges. Use one hand to support the clay and gently ease it into the mould. When fitted beat the clay at the edge of the mould with a wooden spoon to define the rim.

**4** Trim away the excess clay around the rim of the mould with a knife.

**5** Scrape the clay with a serrated metal kidney to get rid of any lumps. Scrape first in one direction and then across in a diagonal direction.

**6** Smooth the surface with the metal kidney until all the marks made by the serrated kidney disappear.

**7** Draw your chosen design on the clay with a needle or pointed tool.

**8** If you make mistakes while drawing the design, you can erase them by rubbing the clay with your finger.

**9** Lift the slab from the mould and gently push from behind to make the design look more three-dimensional. Because of the size and thickness of the slab the press moulded clay will then maintain this form.

**10** Apply the slip to the surface with a brush, then let it dry until it is no longer shiny.

**11** Firmly rub the surface with a smooth pebble as soon as the brushed coating is touch dry. If the slip rubs off leave it to dry for a little longer. Rotate the pebble in small circles or work it in a simple linear way.

**12** If, after the first burnish, you can still see clay underneath, you will need to apply another layer of slip until it is completely covered and you get the desired shine. A final rub with your hands can be given at the near-dry stage. Biscuit (bisque) fire the piece to 1080°C (1976°F). After the firing the surface may lose its burnish but you can restore the shine by applying polishing wax.

# Bas-Relief Tiles

These purple bas-relief tiles were made by Irmin Eggens as a special commission for a bathroom in a Victorian townhouse. Hand-pressing in openback moulds in this way is an effective and fast technique to make small batches of tiles. The repeat moulds were made with a rubber positive cast made from the original plaster mould that was in turn made from the handbuilt clay model.

## Materials
Earthstone clay (or any grogged clay)

## Equipment
Pugcutter or harp (U-shaped rod)
Refuse sacks
Potter's knife
Scrap paper
Rubber kidney
Cardboard
Plaster moulds
Thin short strip of timber
Fork or comb
Small board
2 prepared biscuit (bisque) fired tiles
Brick
Gloves for glazing
Sliptrailer
Sponge
Tile crank
Electric kiln

## Glaze
| | |
|---|---|
| High Alkaline Frit | 76% |
| Potash feldspar | 12% |
| Flint | 10% |
| China clay | 2% |
| Bentonite | 2% |
| Cobalt oxide | 0.3% |
| Copper carbonate | 0.5% |
| Manganese dioxide | 1.5% |

## Firing
Biscuit (bisque) fire to 1180°C (2156°F)
Glaze fire to 1080°C (1976°F) then soak for 20 minutes

**1** Wedge soft clay into a block. The top must be a little bit larger than the tiles. The slabs also have to be slightly higher than the tiles. Cut slabs with a pugcutter or a harp (U-shaped rod).

**2** Place the slabs on a piece of plastic. Cut a template from scrap paper, so that you cut the slabs the right size.

**3** Smooth the surface of each little clay slab with a rubber kidney. The clay will then be better able to pick up fine detailing from the mould.

**4** Place the mould on a piece of cardboard. This makes it easier to move the mould around and avoids damaging the mould and leaving "skid marks" on the workbench. Place the slabs in the middle of the moulds. Work in batches of about 12 to speed up the process.

**5** Press the clay hard into the edges of the mould with both thumbs. Fill as well as possible, so that you leave no air gaps.

**6** Even out the clay with your fist, pressing down firmly. Start at the middle and work towards the edges.

**7** Remove the excess clay with a small piece of timber. Do not use a metal tool for this as it damages the mould. Start from the middle and pull the strip towards you. Do not try to scrape off all the excess clay at once, do it gently in a few strokes. To ensure an absolutely flat back repeat the process diagonally across the mould.

**8** Draw lines at the back of the tile with a fork or a comb while it is still in the mould. It is essential to have such ridges on the underside of wall tiles to make a better grip for adhesive.

**9** Leave the tile for about 30 minutes. Then hold the mould in one hand, place a small board on top covering the back of the tile and turn them over together. Lift up the mould to reveal the tile.

**10** Stack up the wet tiles, face-to-face and back-to-back, between biscuit (bisque) fired tiles and place a brick on top. Turn them occasionally to avoid sticking. Depending on the conditions in your studio they should take about three weeks to dry. Let them dry slowly and evenly to keep them as flat and as straight as possible.

**11** When dry, biscuit (bisque) fire them slowly from 60°C to 600°C (140°F to 1112°F), normal up to 1180°C (2156°F). Do not open the kiln too soon as tiles are very sensitive to thermal shock. Wearing gloves, apply a thick, even layer of transparent glaze with colouring oxides and then wipe each tile back with a damp sponge.

**12** Place the tiles in the individual slots in a tile crank and place them in the kiln. When you make quite a number of tiles it is worth investing in tile cranks to maximize space in your kiln. They are available in different sizes from all good ceramic suppliers. Finally, fire the glazed tiles at 1080°C (1976°F), for 20 minutes.

# St Bride's Box

Soft slabbing, press moulding and hand-modelled decoration are involved in making this elaborate box by Rachel Kneebone. The Church of St Brides in London was the inspiration for the traditional tiered wedding cake, and for this box, evolving from a desire to create an opulent, decadent celebratory piece with a practical function – remember that nothing is "too good to use".

## Materials

Grogged white
    earthenware clay
White slip
Black underglaze
Clear glaze
Lustre: platinum and pink

## Equipment

Newspaper or cloth
Rolling pin
2 guide sticks, approx. 7 mm
    (⅜ in) width
Knife
2 circular templates, 20 cm
    (8 in) and 23 cm (9 in)
    diameter
Cast picture frame mould
    (optional)
3 wooden bats
Brush
Surform blade
Modelling tools
Hand extruder
Face mask (respirator) and
    gloves
Spray gun, booth and
    compressor
Electric kiln

## Glaze

| | |
|---|---|
| Lead sesquisillicate | 75.5% |
| China clay | 18.7% |
| Flint | 5.8% |

## Firing

Biscuit (bisque) fire to 1140°C
    (2084°F)
Lustre fire to 765°C (1409°F)

**1** Roll out three slabs, using the guide sticks to ensure even thickness of clay, which will form the side panel, base and lid of the pot. The side slab should be approximately 16 x 68 cm (6¼ x 27 in). Cut it out with a knife and place to one side. Place the circular templates onto the remaining slabs and cut out. Set all three slabs to one side to dry. It is important to monitor the drying slabs – if the clay dries too much the slabs will crack, if they are too soft they will collapse. To test if a slab is dry enough, curl an edge up as if to form a shape. If it curves easily without distorting, the slab is ready to use. Drying usually takes 15–30 minutes, depending on room temperature.

**2** While the slabs are drying, model the feet – you need six for the base and six for the lid – and the lid handle. You can use a press mould of a picture frame (as shown here) or you can hand model these components.

**3** Place the base slab onto a bat covered with newspaper. Score a ring around the edge of the base slab in readiness to join the side panel. Use the lid template as a guide for positioning. Next, score one side of the side slab. If necessary cut off the excess side slab to permit a clean join. Brush water onto both sets of the scored areas to be joined. Using both hands lift the side slab onto the base slab, curving it to follow the scored ring on the base, then join.

**4** Apply a thin coil of clay over the side and base joins. Work the surfaces with a modelling tool to create a smooth, even finish. Place to one side and leave to dry off until the clay is firm enough to work onto its surface without distorting the form.

**5** Place the lid slab on top of the form. Check that the lid circumference is equal to that of the body. If it is not, use a surform blade to correct. Remove the lid and place it on a separate bat.

**6** Sandwich the pot between two bats and turn it over. Place the six feet for the base an equal distance apart around the edge of the base. Mark their positions and score and slurry the base and bottom of the feet where they will join. Apply the feet and add a thin coil around each join. Leave to harden until the feet can support the weight. Repeat to attach the six feet for the lid. Again, leave to harden until the feet can support the lid's weight.

**7** Turn the lid onto its feet. Extrude coils to ring the side edge of the lid and its rim. Score and slurry around the edge and rim of the lid and apply the coils.

**8** Indent the coils at regular intervals to create a convoluted edge using a modelling tool.

**9** Position the handle in the centre of the lid and mark its position with a knife. Score and slurry the surface of the lid and base of the handle and apply the handle to the lid. Roll a thin coil and smooth on to reinforce the join. Model four roses and eight leaves. Score and slurry the join areas, then apply the roses and leaves to the lid. Place it to one side to dry.

**10** Turn the pot onto its feet. Mark out and score the loops around the top edge of the form, the diagonal side coils and the bottom edge where it joins the base. Start with the top loops and mark an even number, as the design alternates of single and grouped roses. Start the side diagonal score lines at the beginning of each top loop and end at the base of the pot parallel with the end point of the same top loop. Finally score and slurry around the bottom of the pot edge. Attach coils following the marked areas.

**11** Indent the diagonal and base coils with the modelling tool. Leave the top loops smooth. Model the roses and leaves. Score and slurry the areas where the top loops meet and the diagonal side coils cross, and apply the roses and leaves. Tidy up the joined areas with the modelling tool. Leave to dry off.

**12** Remove the lid and place it onto a bat. Wearing a face mask (respirator) and gloves, cover the inner and outer surface of the lid and body with white slip using the spray gun. Wait until the slip is dry before replacing the lid onto the body. Leave the pot and lid in place to dry completely and then biscuit (bisque) fire together.

**13** After firing, paint black underglaze onto the edge of the lid, lid feet, handle, side coils and rose leaves. Spray clear glaze over the inner and outer body, the top and under the surface of the lid. Wash the glaze off the base and the handle feet. Glaze fire the pot with the lid and body separate. Invert the body to paint platinum lustre on the feet and turn to finish the base. Paint pink lustre onto all the other decoration. The black underglaze alters the pink lustre to a pink/gold during the firing.

# Toy Box

The toys Josie Warshaw chose to include in this piece are some of the favourites from her son's toy box. Slabbed, assembled components are used and colour is applied in conjunction with paper-resist decoration. The leatherhard slabs used in this frame can be adapted to any subject.

## Materials
50% T-material clay
50% White Earthenware

## Equipment
Rolling pin
Wooden boards
Knife
Ruler
Stiff brush for slurry
Surform blade
Hacksaw blade
Metal kidney
Flat-ended wooden
    modelling tool
Plastic sheet
Paper
Scissors
Sponge
Newspaper
Gloves for glazing
Latex resist paintbrushes
Black ceramic pencil
Electric kiln

## Glaze
ENGOBE
Ball clay                50%
China clay             20%
Borax frit              50%
COLOUR ADDITIONS
Black stain          8–10%

## Firing
Biscuit (bisque) fire to 1000°C
    (1832°F)
Glaze fire to 1115°C (2039°F)

**1** Roll out sufficient slabs and leave them to become leatherhard. Once the slabs are firm enough not to buckle, cut and butt join them onto a base slab to make up the double wall of the frame. To make a butt join angle the piece at the bottom of the frame by making a chamfered cut to the edge.

**2** Slope the walls of the frame to give a receding feel to the overall shape. Trim the top edges with a surform blade to make a level joining surface for the top slab to contact.

**3** Use slabs that are firm enough not to sag when used for the top slab or "lid" of the frame. Join them into place then cut away the excess of each top slab with a knife. Pare and clean the joins and surfaces.

**4** Leave the frame to firm and even out to leatherhard. Trim the base and pare and clean the entire surface of the frame using a hacksaw blade, metal kidney and flat-ended, wooden modelling tool to clean up the corners. Cover the leatherhard frame and remaining slabs in plastic to prevent them becoming dry.

**5** Place a piece of paper on the inside face of the box then draw the dinosaur on it to get a correct fit. Use the paper template to cut the dinosaur from a leatherhard slab.

**6** Make the train stage-set style, without a back. Use a soft-to-leatherhard slab to make the curve of the roof and engine compartment and the prepared leatherhard slabs to make the other parts.

**7** Make the barrel of the pop gun by rolling soft slabs to form tubes. Leave them to become leatherhard before joining the parts together. Do the finer modelling and finishing once the toy joins become firm again.

**8** Join the toy parts to the main frame, slurrying and scoring the pieces and attaching the bevelled faces. Bevel the edge of the dinosaur shape using a hacksaw blade before joining it in place on the inner face of the box. Clean the joins of excess slurry and fill the gaps with soft clay using a modelling tool and a damp sponge.

**9** Mask the assembled components with newspaper in selected areas to retain the white colour of the clay. Score sharp lines into the clay with a knife tip then start to paint the applied colour. Use dampened newspaper to make clean edges to the areas of applied colours. Lay the engobes using flat brushes and build them up in two layers to make an opaque, evenly laid covering. Leave the box to dry before biscuit (bisque) firing.

**10** After the biscuit (bisque) firing apply latex-resist to the areas selected to retain the colour of the white clay. When the latex is dry apply a wash of black stain to the surface of the work to pick up the scored lines, edges of the paper-resist and incidental surface texture.

**11** Remove the latex-resist and sponge away areas of black stain on the dinosaur spots to give a soft edge. Use black ceramic pencil to draw suggested leaves on the inside face. Fire the work again to 1115˚C (2039˚F).

# Printed Plate

Maria Donato starts her drawings by juxtaposing photocopies of Brazilian Indian graphics, contemporary media and photographs. The images are then manipulated by changing their scale or by photocopying different images on the same piece of paper, such as tracing paper, coloured or textured paper or acetate. This process makes it possible to layer the images, creating a subtle balance of hiding and revealing in the design. These images are then transferred to clay using printmaking processes.

## Materials
T-material clay

## Equipment
Linocut (linoleum board)
Tracing paper
Linocutting tool
Brush
Rolling pin
Gloves for glazing
Screen (wooden frame with a
   fine mesh stretched over it)
Squeegee
Plaster mould
Sponge
Potter's knife
Piece of clear glass with taped
   edges for monoprinting
Ceramic tissue paper
Pencil, ballpoint pen or chalks
Acetate
Ceramic crayons
Soft foam roller
Pre-covercoated decal paper
Scissors
Diluted water-based glue
Rubber kidney
Electric kiln

## Glaze
Underglaze powder mixed
   with water-based medium
Mars Violet pigment mixed
   with screen-printing
   medium
Artic White covercoat
   opaque underglaze
Black body stain and borax frit
   diluted with water
Onglaze powder mixed with
   screen-printing medium

**1** Transfer a design you have selected onto lino by using tracing paper or drawing directly onto the lino. Cut out the chosen image. Paint the lino with underglaze mixed with a water based medium, covering the whole surface with the paint.

**2** Roll a clay slab to the desired thickness. Cut the slab following the shape of the plaster mould, leaving enough clay to be pressed into the mould. Position the clay at the edge of the linocut (linoleum board).

**3** Place the rolled clay over the linocut to print and emboss the image. Repeat this with the clay in a slightly different position to create a juxtaposition of images.

## Firing
Biscuit (bisque) fire to 1180°C
(2156°F)
Final firing to 700–720°C
(1292–1328°F)

**4** Peel off the clay gently to avoid tearing, and allow the surface to become dry to the touch. Note that it is advisable to wear gloves whenever working with ceramic colour.

**5** Apply the printing ink made from Mars Violet pigment mixed with the screen-printing medium to the top of the screen, spreading it evenly. Pull the squeegee firmly and evenly across the whole width of the image on the clay. Lift the screen gently to avoid damaging the surface. Remember to ensure good ventilation in the room where you are working.

**6** Wait until the surface is dry to the touch, but remember that clay should be kept plastic for easy pressing into the mould. Transfer the printed slab of clay into a plaster mould with the patterned surface uppermost. Gently ease the clay into the mould by using a damp clean sponge. Trim the edges from the rim.

**7** Paint on a thin layer of white underglaze to make the printed image opaque, continuing to develop this theme of layering and creating a surface that suggests memories and distant images.

**8** Paint the surface of the glass with the mixture of black body stain and borax frit diluted in water. Allow the mixture to dry. Cover the painted glass with ceramic tissue paper. The paper is sensitive and will pick up marks from your fingers. Tape the tissue paper onto the glass to prevent it from moving. Draw another image onto the tissue paper using a pencil, ballpoint pen or chalks, depending on the type of line you desire.

**9** Photocopy this image onto acetate. This will allow you to position the image where you would like it to be printed so that you can visualize your design before printing it. This technique can be very useful when you are using an intricate design.

**10** To make the print, place your drawing face down onto the damp surface. Printing will not occur if the surface is dry. Rub gently, but firmly, all over the drawing to transfer the image. Peel off the paper.

**11** Remove the piece from the mould and place it face down on a large piece of foam. Smooth the curved surface and paint it using blue and then white underglaze. Paint thin layers allowing each layer to dry before applying the next one. Use ceramic tissue paper and ceramic crayon to create rubbings from the natural form.

**12** Transfer the design onto the damp curved surface using a soft foam roller. Biscuit (bisque) fire the work in an electric kiln to 1180°C (2156°F).

**13** Use onglaze ceramic colour mixed with screen-printing medium to print the next image on the decal. Use pre-covercoated paper to reduce any exposure to fumes. Remember to ensure good ventilation in the room. See step 5 for printing method.

**14** Allow the printed image on the decal paper to dry. Place the paper in warm water until the plastic sheet with the print loosens from the paper. Cover the surface of the biscuit (bisque) fired work with a very diluted water-based glue to prevent the decal from peeling off when drying. This is not necessary if the surface is glazed. Place the decal near the surface to be decorated and then slide off the back paper. Gently place the image in the correct position.

**15** Place the decal over the surface to produce the required design. Firm the decal into place with a rubber kidney, making sure that no water or air pockets are left underneath the covercoat surface. Fire the work to 700°C (1292°F) in a well-ventilated electric kiln – the plastic will burn away leaving the printed design on the ceramic surface. Repeat this process of applying decal and firing until you have the surface decoration you require.

# Raku Squirrel Teapot

A particular feature of Jola Spytkowska's work is manipulating and curving thin slabs of clay into three-dimensional forms so that moulds do not have to be used. Human and animal personalities are sourced from the objects around her – a box of junk can inspire many a hybrid creature to emerge. In this design, sketches of an old oil can and photos of squirrels combine to make an unusual teapot. The raku firing gives a dramatic and spontaneous effect.

## Materials
White St Thomas clay

## Equipment
Box of junk
Sketchbook
Pencil and colour pens
Potter's knife
Toothbrush
Sponge
Wooden board
Rolling pin
Thin card (cardboard)
Scissors
Wooden dowel
Wooden tool
Needle for air holes
Paintbrushes
Thick leather gloves
Protective goggles
Gas bottle (propane tank)
Purpose-made tongs
Large metal bucket
Sawdust
Wire wool
Electric kiln with controller
Raku kiln, gas fired, made
   with refractory kiln bricks

## Glaze
Pre-bought brush-on
   earthenware glazes

## Firing
Biscuit (bisque) fire to 1080°C
   (1976°F)
   60°C (140°F)
   300°C (572°F)
   120°C (248°F)
   1000°C (1976°F)
Glaze fire to 990–1040°C
   (1814–1904°F)

**1** This squirrel was evolved with close reference to drawn designs. If you decide to work in this way, create a drawing of the piece first, which you can refer to throughout the making process. Next, take two balls of clay and pinch out two bowls of equal size. When they have stiffened, even up the edges, score and slurry them (see Handbuilding, using slurry for joining slabs) and join together firmly. Smooth and blend the join.

**2** Cut out two circles from the sphere, a larger one at the base and a smaller one at the top. Prepare a small slab of clay for the teapot base and, when it is stiff, join by scoring and slurrying it to the base so the teapot sits flat. Now work out the dimensions for the head, tail and thighs. Then refer to your drawing and observe the shapes for these.

**3** Make rough templates using thin slabs of clay. Shape and curve them accordingly. Flatten these out again and place onto card. Draw out and cut round the templates. Prepare a large slab of thin clay, place the card templates on it and cut out two of each shape.

**4** Prepare the tail, the head, the ears and eyes, the shoulders, the feet and the thighs. Shape each piece by curving or folding it over a dowel or pressing it into the palm of your hand or into any suitable object. Assemble the components in one place and wait for the clay to stiffen up before joining them.

**5** Join the two halves of the tail and the head. Score and slurry both sides thoroughly. Press together firmly. Smooth the joins, emphasizing them for an added feature. Join the head to the body, then join the tail to the body. This will establish the front and the back of the teapot.

**6** Now that the head and tail are in position, place the shoulders and thighs in between. Make air holes in all of them to avoid explosions in the kiln.

**7** Pinch out a small ball of clay to make the lid using a template for approximate size. To make the flange, roll out a short coil, flatten it lightly and then join it to the underneath of the lid. Coil and roll out small balls of clay to prepare the features for the top of the lid.

**8** Join the features to the lid of the teapot.

**9** Attach the ears and eyes. Impress the eyes with a tool to create the pupils. Then attach the feet.

**10** Prepare the spout for the pot. Take a very thin slab of clay, about 2.5 cm (1 in) wide at one end and 1 cm (½ in) at the other end. Wrap it around a paintbrush, join the edges and then lightly roll the whole thing to blend the join. Carefully remove the paintbrush.

**11** Make a hole in the mouth, otherwise the spout will not pour. Slightly curve the spout before attaching it. Next, biscuit (bisque) fire the squirrel. Outline the edges with a pencil (this will burn away in the raku firing) to identify areas that are to remain unglazed. Unglazed areas will smoke to a charcoal black once in the sawdust.

**12** Refer to your drawing and choose an earthenware, coloured glaze. These glazes fire to a low temperature, which makes them suitable for raku. Apply the glaze with three flowing coats of each colour. When you have finished, fire the squirrel in a gas-fired raku kiln. When the temperature reaches 1000°C (1832°F), remove the kiln lid and lift out the squirrel with purpose-made tongs. Place it in a metal bucket full of sawdust and leave it to smoke for about 20–30 minutes. Remove it and allow it to cool before cleaning and scrubbing gently with wire wool.

# Lady Daisy Jug

This press-moulded and sprigged crystalline-glazed jug (pitcher) for Kate Malone assumes the character of a fine, strong young lady. For her, jugs are a symbol of celebration and sharing and are used at gatherings and to mark special occasions. The original piece from which the mould was made was hand coiled. One new mould can be used to press perhaps 20–30 different jugs. This jug's restrained surface shows the shape of the jug with clarity.

## Materials
T-material clay

## Equipment
Two-piece plaster of Paris
    mould made from coiled
    original body shape
Metal serrated-edge kidney
Thick rubber kidney
Craft knife
Sponge
Plastic sheet
Hacksaw blades of varying
    tooth size
Two-piece plaster of Paris
    handle mould made from
    carved original clay handle
    shape
Banding wheel
Sprig mould of daisy (cast
    from child's earring)
Electric kiln and controller
Large mop-head brush
Gloves for glazing

## Glazes
GREEN CRYSTALLINE GLAZE,
ADAPTED FROM EMMANUEL
COOPER BASE GLAZE

| | |
|---|---|
| Alkaline frit P2962 | 58 g |
| Zinc oxide | 23 g |
| Flint | 17 g |
| Bentonite | 2 g |
| Red iron oxide | 3 g |
| Copper carbonate | 2 g |

CREAMY YELLOW-GOLD HEAVY
BLANKET CRYSTALLINE GLAZE,
ADAPTED FROM A DEREK
CLARKSON BASE GLAZE

| | |
|---|---|
| Ferro frit 3110 | 44 g |
| Zinc oxide | 26.5 g |
| Flint | 20.4 g |
| Titanium dioxide | 7.8 g |
| China clay | 1.4 g |
| Ceramatech high firing colour | 2 g |

## Firing
Biscuit (bisque) fire to 1000°C
    (1832°F)
GLAZE FIRING
60°C (140°F) per hour up to
    180°C (356°F)
80°C (176°F) per hour to
    300°C (572°F)
100°C (212°F) per hour to
    600°C (1112°F)
Then as fast as possible
    to 1260°C (2300°F)
Then cool as fast as possible
    down to 1090°C (1994°F)
Soak there for 90 minutes
Then cool to 1080°C
    (1976°F)
Hold for 60 minutes
Cool to 1069°C (1956°F)
Hold 45 minutes
Turn off kiln for normal cool

**1** Roll out or wire-cut enough slabs of clay to patchwork fill the mould. Lay them in small pieces, filling the mould like crazy paving, overlapping and joining the edges well. This ensures an even, unstretched layer of clay.

**2** Work the inside first with a metal kidney and then a rubber kidney to ensure segment bonding and create a smooth interior. You need to perfect the insides now because this will be too difficult when the two halves are joined. Score and slurry the edges to be joined. A good bonding is crucial.

**3** Push the two halves of the mould and clay together. Work inside the central seam now, scratching, filling and smoothing. The piece should be as beautiful inside as it is outside.

**4** Lie the jug on its side and carefully remove half of the mould leaving the piece created in one half.

**5** Scratch and fill the joint area. Use water from a brush then re-scratch to build a slurry from the body itself.

**6** Fill, but do not overfill, as this creates more work for removal later. The seams between the sections are now strong.

**7** Lift the whole jug from the mould and complete the scratching and filling, paying particular attention to the seam where the two halves join. Wrap it well in plastic and leave for at least 24 hours so the moisture becomes even throughout. It is very difficult to perfect the surface of an unevenly moist piece.

**8** Clean back the pot surface to a perfect, smooth shape by using a series of hacksaw blades from coarse to fine.

**9** Finish off with a rubber kidney, moving it in long, firm sweeps over the form. This stage can take up hours of time so be patient.

**10** Fill both halves of the handle mould. The hollow centre must be clear to avoid an explosion in the kiln. Score and slurry the seams before joining both halves.

**11** Remove the handle from the mould. Check the hollow channel is clear all the way through by making a hole at each end and blowing down the handle.

**12** Scratch and fill the join then wrap it in plastic and leave it to even thoroughly. Next work with hacksaw blades and kidney to perfect the surface.

**14** Press out a few daisy sprigs from the mould.

**13** Put the main jug form on the banding wheel and then join the handle to the body when they are both of the same firmness by scoring and slurrying the contact areas and pushing them together firmly. Put a hand inside of the jug and press against it. If necessary, use a temporary pillar of clay to support the handle.

**15** Join them to the pot on scratched, wet areas and bond them well by even pressure. Wrap the whole piece in plastic and leave to even the moisture for a week. Dry very slowly, especially at the start. Biscuit (bisque) fire in an electric kiln to 1000°C (1832°F).

**16** Glaze the inside by pouring in the glaze, swirling it around. Glaze the outside by painting with a large mop-head brush. Crystalline glazes run during firing so apply about three times as much glaze towards the top than at the base.

The raw glaze is so thick it might crack and fall off in chunks when placing in the kiln so take care. Each pot must have its own homemade kiln prop and tray to collect glaze drips during firing. After firing, chisel the pot from its stilt and polish the base. With luck, crystals will have formed on the surface of the pot, which will have grown during the cooling and soaking cycle of the firing.

# Slim Raku Vessels

Here, Kate Schuricht combines the batch production process of slipcasting with the more individual effects of raku firing. Raku is a fast firing and cooling process whereby glazed pieces are taken out of a kiln when the glaze is molten and placed into sawdust to cool. The result is a distinctive black crackle in the surface of the glaze and smoking of the unglazed body.

## Materials

Casting slip (earthenware)
Molochite grog (80s/120s)

## Equipment

Sieves (60, 80, 120 mesh)
Plaster moulds for slipcasting
Bands to hold moulds
Plastic jugs for slip
Fettling knife
Natural sponges
Electric kiln for biscuit
    (bisque) firing
Potter's knife
Plastic bowls
Gas cylinder (propane tank)
Burner with regulator
Raku kiln (oil drum lined with
    ceramic fibre, brick-lined
    gas kiln etc.)
Metal raku tongs
Thick leather gloves
Protective goggles
Sawdust
Bricks for the sawdust pit
Metal lid
Wire wool

## Glaze

BASE TRANSPARENT GLAZE
Soft borax frit          85%
China clay               15%
Add oxides and stains

## Firing

Biscuit (bisque) fire to 1000°C
    (1832°F)
Raku fire to 900–920°C
    (1652–1688°F), using
    spyhole to check glaze

**1** Prepare the casting slip. Add between 15–25% grog to the slip, stirring well and sieving the mix before use. Put the plaster moulds together and secure with a strong band. Pour in the grogged, sieved slip to the top of the mould and top up as necessary during the casting period. Gently tap the filled mould and rock slightly to release any trapped air bubbles from the slip.

**2** Allow the pieces to cast for approximately 20 minutes for a medium thickness, then pour the slip out and leave to drain at a slight angle for a further 20–30 minutes until the surface of the slip is firm to the touch. Turn the moulds upright and allow the casts to dry a little longer. When the cast is firm enough cut away the spare with a moist fettling knife. Sponge back using a damp sponge to refine edges and remove any marks. Gently remove the cast from the mould – it should drop out quite easily.

**3** Fettle the slipcast forms when leatherhard, using a fettling knife and a moist natural sponge to refine the surface and smooth out any bumps. Leave the pieces to dry completely before biscuit (bisque) firing them to approximately 1000°C (1832°F). Firing them too high will mean that the clay body will become less resistant to thermal shock.

**4** Lightly sponge the surface of the biscuit (bisque) fired piece with a damp sponge to ensure that it is free from dust and grease. Stir the glaze thoroughly before sieving through an 80, and then a 120 mesh sieve. Stir it regularly to avoid settling. Pour the glaze into the top or rim of the piece and then pour out leaving a layer roughly 1 mm thick. Carefully scratch through the glaze with a potter's knife to test the thickness. Clean up the edges and rims.

**5** Dip the piece into the first glaze for a few moments and remove, allowing the moisture to be absorbed. Dip into a second glaze and leave for a couple of seconds (optional). Clean off roughly 3 mm (⅛ in) of glaze at the bases in case it runs. Leave any surfaces that touch the kiln shelf glaze free. Leave the pieces to dry overnight before firing.

**6** Place the shelves into the base of the kiln at a level just above the burner hole. Load the pieces onto the shelves with enough room between each one to allow the tongs to move freely when unloading. It is best to ensure at this stage that a glazed surface will be in sight when you look into the spy hole during firing. Put on the extension rings followed by the lid.

**7** Light the burner on a low flame to start with, until all the moisture is driven out of the pieces, and then step up the kiln at regular intervals (roughly every 15 minutes). A firing can take anything from 40 minutes to an hour and a half. After firing for about 30–40 minutes, the glazes will start to melt and will appear bubbly and slightly matt in texture. The glaze will then flatten out and mature, becoming shiny and smooth. When you can see a good reflection from the glaze surface, the kiln will be ready to unload.

**8** Turn off the gas supply from the bottle, then the regulator, and finally the burner itself, waiting until all the gas has burnt out of the hose. This stops gas becoming trapped in the hose, which can be dangerous. Wearing gloves and goggles, remove the kiln lid and extension rings and place them on bricks on the ground, away from anything combustible.

**9** The sawdust pit needs to be close to the kiln to allow for speedy unloading. There should be a layer of sawdust in the bottom of the pit and enough to cover the pieces. The sawdust needs to be slightly damp to stop it from bursting into flames, but not too wet that it stops it from smoking. Have a bucket of water to hand in case of emergency. Remove the pieces quickly and carefully, holding the metal raku tongs with the heat resistant gloves. Keep calm to avoid unnecessary breakage and injury. At this stage in the firing your pots will come alive and all the characteristic crackles and smokiness will occur.

**10** Carefully place the pieces into the pit ensuring they do not touch. Cover quickly with plenty of sawdust until no smoke can be seen. You will need at least one helper for better and quicker covering. Cover with a final layer of sawdust and a lid (ideally metal) to stop the pots from cooling too fast.

**11** Leave the pieces to cool in the sawdust for 15 minutes to one hour. Check the pit regularly in case the sawdust catches fire. If possible, leave the pots in the pit until they are cool enough to remove with gloves. They can cool in the air or can be quenched in water.

**12** Once the pieces are cool enough to handle, place them in water to remove the black deposit on the glaze. This can be easily removed by gently rubbing with your fingers, but you may need to use wire wool on some areas. Dry the pieces thoroughly after washing as they are porous. This means that raku-fired pieces are not watertight and are not suitable for use with food or drink.

# Lidded Boxes

This project combines the techniques of slipcasting with raku, and here Kate Schuricht uses the form of a small, lidded, slipcast box that is glazed with a different glaze on the inside and outside. The application of glaze aims to achieve a uniform finish, which draws attention to the distinctive pattern of the crackles over the form created by the raku firing.

## Materials
Casting slip (earthenware)
Molochite grog (80s/120s)

## Equipment
Sieves (60, 80, 120 mesh)
Plaster moulds for slipcasting
Bands to hold moulds together
Plastic jugs for slip
Fettling knife
Natural sponges
Electric kiln
Potter's knife
Plastic bowls
Measuring jugs
Tray or container
Glaze claw (optional)
Metal kidney (rectangular)
Gas cylinder (propane tank)
Burner with regulator
Raku kiln
Metal raku tongs
Thick leather gloves
Protective goggles
Sawdust
Bricks for the sawdust pit
Metal lid
Wire wool

## Glaze
BASE TRANSPARENT GLAZE
Soft borax frit          85%
China clay               15%
Add oxides and stains

## Firing
Biscuit (bisque) fire to 1000°C
   (1832°F)
Raku fire to 900–920°C
   (1652–1688°F) – use
   spyhole to check.

**1** Cast the box with grogged casting slip, being sure to agitate the mould initially to get rid of any air bubbles. Cast for approximately 20 minutes then pour out the slip, draining the moulds diagonally to ensure a clean drain. Leave to drain upside down at a slight angle for a further 20 minutes.

**2** Wait for the casts to become firm, then trim the spares from the casts using a fettling knife and a moist, natural sponge to smooth off the cut edges.

**3** Remove the lid and box casts from the moulds, placing the lid onto the box to dry. The lid will act as a setter for the box by preventing it from warping. Fettle the cast when leatherhard and sponge away any marks with a natural sponge. Once dry, biscuit (bisque) fire the box to approximately 1000°C (1832°F) with the lid still on.

**4** Next, sponge the surface of the bisqueware with a moist, natural sponge to remove any dirt or dust. Pour the raku glaze into the inside of the box and pour out. Leave a margin of about 5 or 6 mm (¼ in) free from glaze so the lid can be placed on without the glazed surfaces touching and sticking during firing. For the best results, leave the glaze to dry before glazing the outside. Dip the outside of the box into a tray or container of glaze, holding it carefully with your fingers or a glaze claw.

**5** Check to see that the glaze has dried enough to touch, then wearing a face mask (respirator) scrape the glaze off the bottom of the box with a metal kidney, scraping all the dry glaze back into the glaze bucket to be used again. Use the same dipping method for glazing the lid. Clean the glaze to a level of approximately 2 mm (¹⁄₁₂ in) around the base of the box to allow for the glaze to run when firing. Place the bases directly onto the kiln shelf for firing.

**6** Load the kiln leaving adequate space between boxes to allow for free movement of the tongs during unloading. It is a good idea when firing lidded containers in the raku kiln to keep the lids on. The forms will then be less likely to warp in the direct heat from the burner and there will be more room on the kiln shelves for the pieces. Put on the kiln lid, ignite the burner on low to start the firing, stepping up at regular intervals of about 15 minutes.

**7** Fire for between 45 minutes to one hour. Once the kiln has reached full temperature and you can see through the spyhole that the glaze is molten with a shiny, smooth surface, put on the leather gloves and protective goggles and unload the kiln using the tongs to hold the boxes in the middle.

**8** Place the boxes carefully into the sawdust pit, making sure that the glazed surfaces do not touch.

**9** Quickly and carefully remove the lid from the box before covering with sawdust. This allows the sawdust to reach the inside of the box and burn carbon into the crackles. Continue to cover the pieces with sawdust until no smoke can be seen, then cover the pit with a galvanised metal lid and leave the pieces to cool for about an hour if possible.

**10** When the boxes are cool, remove them from the sawdust pit and place them into water to clean. Use wire wool to gently remove the carbon from the surface of the glaze. Rinse off and allow the pieces to dry completely in the air. Although the pieces are glazed, they will not hold water and should be considered as decorative pieces only.

# SUPPLIERS AND SERVICES

For local sources, check your local telephone directory, as well as advertisements in ceramic magazines.

## United Kingdom

**BRITISH CERAMIC TESTING
RESEARCH LTD**
Tel 01782 764444
*Glaze testing services*

**BRITISH PLASTER BOARD**
Newark Works
Bowbridge Lane, Newark
Nottingham NG24 3BZ
Tel 01636 678206; Fax 01636 673542
*Will advise on a local outlet for plaster*

**BRITTAINS (TR) LTD**
Ivy House Paper Mills,
Commercial Road, Hanley
Stoke on Trent
Staffordshire ST1 3QS
Tel 01782 202 567;
Fax 01782 202157
*Decal paper and pottery tissue*

**CERAMATECH LTD**
Units 16 & 17, Frontier Works
33 Queen Street,
London N17 8JA
Tel 020 8885 4492;
Fax 020 8365 1563
*Equipment, clay, glazes, etc*

**CP CERAMICS**
37 Buxton Street, London E1 5HE
Tel 020 7247 4223;
Fax 020 7377 0311
*Ceramic model and mould making*

**VJ GOODHALLS**
Barker Street, Longton
Stoke on Trent
Staffordshire ST3 1PE
Tel 01782 319 696
*Jigger and jolley services, cup heads,
metal back shapes*

**JOHNSTONE MATTHEY**
Colour and Print Division,
Cresswell Road, Stoke onTrent
Staffordshire ST11 9RD
Tel 01782 388399; Fax 01782 388303
*Colours and inks*

**KINGFISHER CERAMICS**
Scapa Filtration, Heathcote Works
Burslem, Stoke on Trent
Staffordshire ST6 4EQ
Tel 01782 575254; Fax 01782 575237
*Mouldmaking equipment*

**LONGTON LIGHT ALLOYS**
Foxley Lane, Milton, Stoke on Trent
Staffordshire ST2 7HE
Tel 01782 536615; Fax 01782 533415
*Hollow extrusion die plates*

**JOHNSON MATTHEY**
Ceramics and Materials Ltd,
Woodbank Street, Burslem
Stoke on Trent
Staffordshire ST6 3AT
Tel 01782 524949; Fax 01782 524950
*Glazes and colour*

**PAMELA MORETON**
22B Holt Road, Cromer
Norfolk NR27 9JW
Tel 01263 512629
*Decal printing service*

**RICHARD PHETHEAN**
The Leadenporch House
New Street, Deddington
Banbury, Oxon OX1 OSP
Tel 01869 338791
*Throwing tuition and ceramic workshops*

**STEPHEN WEBSTER PLASTICS**
Brick Knoll Park, Ashley Road
St Albans, Herts AL1 5PL
Tel 01727 863138
*Cottles for mouldmaking*

## United States

**AMACO**
4717 West 16th Street
Indianopolis, Indiana 46222
Tel 317 244 6871
*Equipment, clay, glazes, etc*

**AXNER POTTERY SUPPLY**
P O Box 1484 Oviedo,
Florida 32765
Tel 407 365 1858
*Equipment, clay, glazes, etc*

**BIO-TECHNICS LABORATORIES**
1133 Crenshaw Boulevard
Los Angeles, CA 90019
Tel 323 933 5991
*Glaze testing services*

**KENTUCKY TENNESSEE CLAY CO**
Box 6002, Mayfield
Kentucky 42066
Tel 502 247 3061
*Equipment, clay, glazes, etc*

**LAGUNA CLAY CO**
East Coast: 4022 Mill Road
Skaneateles,
New York 13152
Tel 315 685 8378
*Equipment, clay, glazes, etc*

**MINNESOTA CLAY CO**
8001 Grand Avenue South
Bloomington, Minnesota 55420
Tel 612 884 9101
*Equipment, clay, glazes, etc*

**SOLDNER POTTERY**
PO Box 90, Aspen CO 81612
Tel and fax: 970 925 3742
*Clay mixers and equipment*

**TRINITY CERAMIC SUPPLY INC.**
9016 Diplomacy Row, Dallas
Texas 75247
Tel 214 631 0540
*Equipment, clay, glazes, etc*

## Australia

**DIGITEMP**
BPQ Controls, 14 Margaret Street
Beachmere Queensland 4510
Tel 074 962 199; Fax 074 968 238
*Kiln equipment, calibration and repairs*

**NORTHCOTE POTTERY**
85A Clyde Street, Thornbury 3071
Tel 03 480 4799
*Equipment, clay, glazes, etc plus general
tuition and ceramic workshops*

**POTTERS' EQUIPMENT**
13/42 New Street, Ringwood
Victoria 3134
Tel 03 870 7533; Fax 03 879 1799
*Equipment, clay, glazes, etc*

**PUGGOON POTTERY
SUPPLIERS**
P O Box 199, Gulgong, NSW 2852
Tel 063 74 1448
*Equipment, clay, glazes, etc*

**TALISMEN**
221 Macquarie Street, Hobart
Tasmania
Tel 002 23 5536
*Equipment, clay, glazes, etc*

## Canada

**CUPEPPER POTTERY**
700 58th Avenue, SE Calgary Alberta
T2H 2E2

**THEKER POTTERY SUPPLIES**
15 West Pearce Street
Richmond Hill, Ontario L4B 1H6

## New Zealand

**TALISMEN**
124 Rimu Road, Paraparauma
Tel 00 64 58 84377; Fax 00 64 58
73107
*Pottery equipment*

# BIBLIOGRAPHY

## Specialist magazines

**AMERICAN CERAMICS**
9 East 45th Street
New York, NY 10017
USA
Tel 212 661 4397; Fax 212 661 2389
*Published quarterly*

**ARTISTS' NEWSLETTER**
PO Box 23
Sunderland SR4 6DG
United Kingdom
Tel 0191 567 3589
*Analysis, commentary and information across contemporary visual arts, published monthly*

**CERAMIC REVIEW**
21 Carnaby Street
London W1V 1PH
United Kingdom
http://www.ceramic-review.co.uk/
*English based magazine with some international features, published bi-monthly*

**CERAMICS ART & PERCEPTION**
35 William Street, Paddington
NSW 2021
Australia
Tel 02 3615286; Fax 02 3615402
http://www.ceramicart.com.au
*Internationally based magazine, published quarterly*

**CERAMICS MONTHLY**
735 Ceramic Place, PO Box 6102
Westerville, OH 43086
USA
Tel 614 523 1660; Fax 614 891 8960
http://www.ceramicsmonthly.org/
*American and international potters and technique based articles, published monthly*

**NEW ZEALAND POTTER**
Box 881, Auckland
New Zealand
Tel 09 415 9817; Fax 09 309 3247

**THE POTTER'S SHOP**
31 Thorpe Road
Needham Heights, MA
USA
Tel 02494 781 449
*Books and videos*

**POTTERY IN AUSTRALIA**
PO Box 937, Crows Nest
Sydney, NSW 2065
Australia
Tel 02 9901 3353; Fax 02 436 1681
*Some international features, published quarterly*

**THE STUDIO POTTER**
Box 70, Goffstown, NH 03045
USA
Tel 603 774 3542
http://www.studiopotter. org/
*Publishes two journals and two newsletters annually*

**STUDIO POTTERY**
15 Magdalen Road
Exeter EX2 4TA
United Kingdom
Tel 01392 430082; email studio
pottery@mail.inxpress.co.uk
www.inxpress.co.uk/studio.pottery
*English based magazine including articles on individual potters and ceramics in society, published quarterly*

## Advice and help

**CRAFTSMEN POTTERS' ASSOCIATION (CPA)**
William Blake House
Marshall Street,
London W1V 1FD
United Kingdom
Tel 0171 930 4811
*Runs a specialist gallery and publishes annually an illustrated directory of members*

**THE CRAFTS COUNCIL**
44A Pentonville Road, Islington
London
United Kingdom
Tel 0171 278 7700 (Reference
Section 0171 806 2501)
www.craftscouncil.org.uk
*Advice on other regional craft bodies throughout UK. Offers grant assistance and helps in the promotion of work*

**KIK INFORMATION CENTRE FOR CONTEMPORARY CRAFTS**
Kirkegate 1–3,
0130 Oslo
Norway
Tel 22 40 41 30 Fax 22 40 41 31

*Ceramics and Print*; Paul Scott; Black; 1994
*Clay & Glazes for the Potter*; Daniel Rhodes; Pitman; 1957
*The Craft of the Potter*; Michael Casson; BBC; 1977
*The Electric Kiln*; Harry Fraser; Black; 1994
*A Guide to Modern Australian Ceramics*; Janet Mansfield; Craftsman House; 1988
*Hand Built Ceramics*; Jane Waller; Batsford; 1990
*Hands in Clay*; Charlotte Speight and John Toki; Mayfield; 1994
*Hans Coper and Lucie Rie*; Tony Birks; Marston House; 1983 and 1987
*Nature as a Source*; Kim Jacobsen; The Crafts Council; 1995
*Paper Clay*; Rosette Gault; Penn/Black; 1998
*Plastermould and Model Making*; Chaney and Skee; Prentice Hall; 1973
*The Potter's Art*; Garth Clark; Phaidon; 1995
*A Potter's Book*; Bernard Leach; Faber & Faber; 1940
*The Potter's Dictionary of Materials and Glazes*; Frank Hamer; Pitman; 1975
*The Potter's Manual*; Kenneth Clark; Macdonald Orbis; 1983
*Pottery & Ceramics*; Christies; Phaidon; 1984
*Pottery in the Making*; Freestone and Gaimster; British Museum Press; 1977
*Single Firing*; Fran Tristram; Gentle Breeze/Black; 1996
*Slips and Slipware*; Anthony Phillips; Batsford; 1990
*Smashing Pots*; N Barley; British Museum Press; 1994
*Tang and Liao Ceramics*; W Watson; Thames & Hudson; 1984
*World Ceramics*; Hamlyn; 1968

## Further reading

*Ceramics and Print*; Paul Scott; A & C Black; 1994
*Clay and Glazes for the Potter*; D Rhodes, Pitman; 1957
*Clays and Glazes in Studio Ceramics*; David Scott; The Crowood Press; 1998
*Decorated Earthenware*; Mike Levy; Batsford; 1994
*Glazes*; Emmanuel Cooper; Batsford; 1994
*New Ceramic Trends and Traditions*; Peter Dormer; Thames & Hudson; 1986
*The Potter's Directory of Shape Function & Form*; Neal French; Krause; 1998
*The Potter's Palette*; Christine Constant and Steve Ogden; Apple; 1996
*Raku*; Ian Byers; Batsford, 1992
*Single Firing: The Pros and Cons*; Fran Tristram; A & C Black; 1996
*Slips and Slipware*; Anthony Phillips; Batsford; 1990
*Soda Glazing*; Ruthanne Tudball; A & C Black; 1995
*Tin Glazed Earthenware*; Daphne Carnegy; Black/Chilton; 1993

# ACKNOWLEDGEMENTS

## Author's acknowledgements

Many thanks to all those who gave help with the arrangements for photography and to those who have contributed project work.

David Richardson for his contributions and advice regarding plaster working methods. Stephen Brayne for his creative photographic documentation of techniques and project work as well as his fearless exposure to shooting flames and searing heat.

Emma Clegg for giving me this opportunity to consolidate and learn and for always being there on telephone or fax to calmly guide me through the book-making process.

Nigel Hubbers for advice about the use of internet; Steve Rafferty of Ceramatech for swift organising and delivery of materials; Teresa Pateman for the loan of etching plates; Pip Cronin and Jessica Cohen for the use of their studio and equipment; Chris Bramble and Kay Suckling for their preparation work for photography; David Bailey Junior at Longton Light Alloys for their speedy supply of extruding equipment; Iain Ogilvie at Blackthorn Galleries for selling advice; Jonathan Knowles, Yiolanda Christou and Billy Nicholas for kiln watching; Vince Woodrush for backdrop and light; and Maria Donato for supplying printing blocks and equipment.

My thanks are due also to Daphne Carnegy as adviser on glaze technicalities and as book writing mentor; John Forde for acting as consultant; Jenny Lomax and Laurie Peake and the entire Camden Arts centre team past and present for my much enjoyed teaching opportunities and enlightenment.

Many thanks to Dorcas Apoh for entertaining and caring for my son while I met the deadline. And to my partner Peter Norman for all his encouragement and support, as well as help and advice with the keyboard.

## Publisher's acknowledgements

With very many thanks to Josie Warshaw who as well as applying her wide specialist ceramic knowledge has researched, planned, questioned and delivered with conscientious professionalism.

And to all those who contributed the remaining technical sections and projects: Maria Donato (Printed Plate), 22 Kingsgate Workshops, 110–116 Kingsgate Road, London NW6 2JG); Irmin Eggens (Bas-fired Relief Tiles), Janmatthyssenlaan 10, 3232 Ed Brielle, The Netherlands; Rachel Kneebone (St Bride's Box) Glebe Road Studio, 18 Glebe Road, London E8 4BD;

Kate Malone (Lady Daisy Jug), Balls Pond Studio, 8b Culford Mews, London N1 4BX; Sarah Scampton (Full-bellied Coiled Pot) 49 Kingsgate Workshops, 110–116 Kingsgate Road, London NW6 2JG; Kate Schuricht (Slim Raku Vessels and Lidded Boxes) Studio E2M, Cockpit Arts, Cockpit Yard, Northington Street, London WC1N 2NP; Jola Spytkowska (Raku Bug and Raku Squirrel Teapot) c/o Balls Pond Studio, 8b Culford Mews, London N1 4BX; Josie Warshaw (Balancing Tricks, Coiled Snake and Toy Box), 43 Kingsgate Workshops, 110–116 Kingsgate Road, London NW6 2JG; and to Mette Gregesen, Suzanne Lanchbury and Montse Jalon at Camberwell College of Art (Burnished Plate) c/o Ceramics Department, Camberwell College of Art, Peckham Road, London SE5 8UF.

Thanks also to Camberwell College of Art Ceramics Department for allowing us to photograph their equipment, and in particular to John Forde for his assistance and advice.

## Picture Credits

Thank you to the following museums and agencies for permission to reproduce pictures in this book: page 45 (Kari Christensen) KIK, Norway; page 65 (first column) Sabina Teuteberg; page 122–123

And grateful thanks to the following potters who generously lent us actual pieces or photographs of their work for photography and reproduction:
Keith Ashley, Duncan Ayscough, Peter Beard, Jenny Beavan, Liz Beckenham, Alison Britton, Sandy Brown, Deidre Burnett, Kyra Cane, Daphne Carnegy, Michael Casson, Russell Coates, Emmanuel Cooper, Claire Curneen, John Dawson, Mike Dodd, Maria Donato, Margaret Forde, Julie Goodwin, Frank Hamer, Jane Hamlyn, Ewen Henderson, Brendon Hesmondhalgh, Ashley Howard, Philip Jolley, Tavs Jorgensen, Julian King-Salter, Anna Lambert, Peter Lane, Jennifer Lee, Andrew Lord, Gillian Lowndes, Sophie MacCarthy, Fenella Mallalieu, Kate Malone, Bodil Manz, Warren Mather, Pamela Mei Yee Leung, Aki Moriuchi, Emily Myers, Jenny Orchard, Jeff Oestreich, Sue Paraskeva, Colin Pearson, Grayson Perry, Jane Perryman, Nancy Selvage, Ray Silverman, Richard Slee, Rosie Smith, Helen Smythe, Rupert Spira, Kay Suckling, Janice Tchalenko, Neil Tetkowski, Sabina Teuteberg, Judy Trim, Ruthanne Tudball, Prue Venables, Jane Waller, Josie Warshaw, Janet Williams and Tessa Wolfe-Murray.

NOTES

# NOTES

# NOTES